HOW TO GET ALONG WITH ALMOST ANYONE

HOW TO GET ALONG WITH ALMOST ANYONE

A Complete Guide to Building Positive Relationships
with Family, Friends, Co-workers

H. NORMAN WRIGHT

WORD PUBLISHING
Dallas · London · Sydney · Singapore

HOW TO GET ALONG WITH ALMOST ANYONE

Library of Congress Cataloging in Publication Data

Wright, H. Norman.
How to get along with almost anyone / H. Norman Wright.
p. cm.
ISBN 0-8499-0739-X : $12.99
ISBN 0-8499-3256-4 (pbk.)
1. Interpersonal relations. I. Title.
HM132.W75   1989
302—dc20   89-35717
                                                        CIP

2 3 4 5 6 7 8 9 LBM 7 6 5 4

Printed in the United States of America

Contents

HOW TO
GET ALONG
WITH
ALMOST
ANYONE

1

Some People Really Know How to Get Along

"People—that's the problem with the world!" the man in my office said emphatically. "If there weren't any people, we wouldn't have all these problems." His statement sounded strange to me; but he was dead serious. As I reflected on his words, I realized he was verbalizing what many of us have said or thought: Most of our difficulties in life occur because of other people. Life seems to be one continuing challenge of getting along with parents, friends, employers, employees, fellow workers, ministers, parishioners, fiancés, spouses, children, landlords, and all the other people we deal with in our lives. Ever since Adam and Eve, the members of God's human creation have had problems getting along with one another.

Most people really want to get along with those around them. Perhaps you've heard the humorous story of the man who was desperate to improve his relationships. He went to the bookstore and scoured the shelves looking for a book that would help him get along with others. He searched and searched before he finally found a large book with the impressive title, *How to Hug.* From reading the title he was so confident that the book could help him that he rushed to the counter and bought it without even opening it. Upon returning home, he discovered that the book was no help at all. He had purchased volume 9 of an encyclopedia!

For more than twenty-five years in my counseling practice, I've talked to thousands of people who really want to get along with family members, friends, fellow church members, co-workers, and neighbors. Our bookstores are filled with books on the subject of helping people get along with each other. And these books sell well, reflecting the interest and need of the population. But for all the books sold and read, people still have trouble getting along with other people. It's not that they don't know what to do. Information abounds. But most people fail to put the information into practice on a consistent basis.

How is this book different from countless other Christian books offering help for relationship problems? To be honest, many of the suggestions in these pages are not new. You've probably run across many of them before. But I've tried in this book to present these ideas in a way that makes them easy to integrate into your relationships with others. If you're like many Christians, you are better at soaking in than living out. This book of tips and ideas gives you another opportunity to start practicing learnable skills for getting along with people.

I've tried to keep two things in mind as I wrote these chapters. First, I wanted this book to be *practical.* The suggestions you find are not especially profound; but they *are* simple and workable. The clear-cut strategies in this book can be practiced, not just pondered. Over the years, I've seen many lives changed by their consistent application.

As you consider each principle in the chapters to come, ask yourself, "Is this principle already working in my life? If so, who would attest to it? If not, how will I make it happen?" I've talked to many who exclaim, "Oh, I want to be able to do that. I want that quality in my life." But nothing happens. They have great desires and admirable goals, but without a practical plan, their desires and goals die on the vine. Watch for practical strategies for growth in this book, then plan to roll up your sleeves and go to work on adding them to your life.

Second, I wanted this book to be *Bible based.* The finest principles for getting along with people are found in the Word of God. Actually, if people followed the teachings in the Bible, this book and others like it would be unnecessary. God's people-principles work. But getting along with others does not happen simply by practicing some techniques or learning how to behave in a certain manner. Real change must come from within; your heart and your attitude toward people are involved. God's Word must change us on the inside before the practical principles can change us on the outside.

The good news is that we don't need to struggle through our relationships on the power generated by our own motors. We have at our disposal the power and direction of the Holy Spirit for solving our people problems. When we start practicing the presence of the Spirit in our daily interaction with others, our relationships will change for the better. And because God is in them, these changes will last.

The Kind of People Who Get Along

Who are the people you know who appear to get along well with others? What is so special about them? What qualities do they possess which make them people persons? The people I know who get along well with others are enjoyable to be with. They show genuine interest in others. When they are with you, they are really *with you.*

I think of a man I know who is very gracious, friendly, and refined in his dealings with people, whether they are his friends, his co-workers, or the waiters who serve him. His pleasant manner is not put on; it's genuine. And he gets along with almost everybody. When I'm with him, he treats me as an individual. I am accepted for who I am and viewed by him as a person of worth. He listens to me and appreciates my contributions to the conversation.

A man who encourages and builds up others, he is compassionate and empathetic, touching people in times of joy and sorrow. He fits the description of a likable character I read about recently in a novel. This man was described as "large-hearted with everyone." The way my friend treats the people in his life is how most people want to be treated.

Do these qualities describe how you would like to be treated? Are these qualities evident in your dealings with others? It takes time to develop the qualities I find in my friend. I'm still working on them in my life. Fortunately, we all have the capacity to learn them and put them into practice.

Levels of Relationship

As we move through life interacting with relatives, friends, co-workers, and fellow believers, we don't experience the same depth of relationship with everyone. There are several different levels of relationships. For example, you don't have the same kind of relationship with your fellow employees you have with your immediate family. Sometimes the intensity of a relationship is the result of planned activity on our part. For instance, you may purposely cultivate a friendship with a new person at church to make him feel included. But sometimes relationships just happen—when you are drawn to someone who enjoys the same hobby you enjoy, for example. Many factors determine the different levels of relationship we experience with the various people in our lives.

One way to look at relationships is to see them either as *casual* or *binding*. Binding relationships may include those with spouse, parents, children, in-laws and other relatives, bosses and co-workers, or any relationship which is valued as permanent or long term. Casual relationships are those you have with neighbors, distant friends, acquaintances, or anyone you relate to apart from a permanent or long-term commitment. Obligations to binding relationships are—or should be—greater than to casual relationships. Since binding relationships are permanent, there are very few valid reasons for terminating them. However, you may find yourself in a binding relationship, such as with a relative or even your spouse, which is being treated by one or both parties as a casual relationship. The lack of commitment when it is expected can put a great strain on the relationship and cause individuals to get along poorly. Clarifying expectations, especially in binding relationships, is essential to getting along with those closest to you.[1]

There will be some casual relationships in your life that you honestly wish didn't exist. For example, we've all had co-workers who were unpleasant to be around or whom we just didn't "click" with. And we all have some binding relationships that we wish were only casual relationships. We would have no reason to relate to some of our relatives through blood or marriage if a family connection didn't exist. We just don't have much in common. But uncomfortable relationships like these don't need to be irritating or burdensome. We can learn to get along with these people through the dynamic of the presence of Jesus Christ changing our attitudes.

Another strategy is to identify four relationship levels: *minimal, moderate, strong,* and *quality.* Let's look at each one separately.

Minimal relationships. Minimal relationships involve simple, surface-level verbal interaction which is generally pleasant instead of hostile. People in relationships at this level usually do not give or receive help, emotional support, or love from each other. They just speak and listen to each other when it is necessary. You will have a minimal relationship with the people you are uncomfortable around, but with whom you must relate to some degree. The key to getting along in a minimal relationship is to determine in advance how much you need to interact with this person and then strive to make that interaction as healthy as possible.

Who are the people in your life today that fit the classification of minimal relationships? What are your feelings about them at this time? How often do you pray for them and *how* do you pray for them?

Moderate relationships. A moderate relationship contains all the characteristics of a minimal relationship, but includes one more: an emotional attachment. In moderate relationships, you want emotional support and you are willing to give emotional support. There is an openness which enables both parties to listen to each other's hurts, concerns, joys, and needs. Ideally, this openness is a two-way street. But even when it is not, we believers are called to respond with openness regardless of the other person's response.

Emotional support is the foundation upon which deep relationships can be built. For example, a marriage that is not based on an emotional bond between partners will not be a fulfilling marriage. Often we become the catalyst for moderate relationships by taking the initial steps of emotional openness and support. The other person may follow suit or be threatened by our openness. It may be difficult for someone to trust you with held-back emotions because of prior hurts in his or her life. Then all you can do is take the risk to be open and reach out. It's all right for people to move slowly toward emotional openness. Moderate relationships take time to build.

Who are the people in your life today who fit the classification of moderate relationships? What are your feelings about them? How often do you pray for them and how do you pray for them?

Strong relationships. The difference between a moderate relationship and a strong one is found in the word *help.* Strong relationships develop when you really become involved with people by reaching out to minister to them in tangible ways. You're ready to provide help when they need it, and you accept help from them when you need it.

For some people, the helping aspect of a strong relationship is easier than the emotional aspect. In fact, many people bypass the emotional attachment in their relationships and focus just on helping. The personal investment is less; and yet, strong relationships *must* be based on emotional support for the caring to be meaningful. Short-circuiting emotional support leads to shallow relationships. Emotional support is a stronger tie than helping.

Who are the people in your life today who fit the classification of strong relationships? What are your feelings about them at this time? How often do you pray for them and how do you pray for them?

Quality relationships. All the elements of the previous levels lead to the deepest level of all: quality relationships. Quality relationships include the added element of loving trust. You feel safe with these people when you reveal to them your inner needs, thoughts, and feelings. You also feel free to invite them to share their inner needs, thoughts, and feelings—and they feel safe in doing so. Quality relationships can exist between friends, spouses, parents, children, and even co-workers. There are no secrets and no barriers. The relationship is built upon complete mutual trust.

What people in your life today fit the classification of quality relationships? How do you feel about them at this time? How often do you pray for them and how do you pray for them?[2]

Why Relationships Fail

Getting along with others involves all the dynamics of relationships at their different levels. Not all relationships succeed. Why do some fail? I think there are two basic reasons, which may be expressed in many different ways.

The first reason is *fear*. We are fearful people, often driven more by fear than by hope. And when we live by fear, we erect barriers, act and react defensively, and fail to be open and trusting with others. Relationships ruled by fear are in danger of failing.

The second reason is *selfishness*. Relationships—especially binding relationships—revolve around need fulfillment. Focusing on fulfilling the needs of others is the best way to get along with them. But often selfishness butts in and we focus instead on fulfilling our own needs ahead of the needs of others.

In premarital counseling, I ask the man and woman to identify in writing their personal requirements and specify how they would like their future spouse to meet those needs. We then evaluate the lists to determine a realistic plan for behavior. Sometimes, after one has shared his or her list of needs, the partner will complain, "Hey, what about my needs? I'll have to spend so much time meeting your needs that my needs will never be met!"

This is the common inner cry of selfish people today: "I want my needs met first." But there is only one really good way to get your needs met: by meeting the needs of others. I don't mean that you must be a martyr, a victim, or a passive, compliant nonentity in the relationship. Simply focus on obeying scripture: "Do nothing from selfishness or empty conceit, but with humility of mind let each of you regard one another as more important than himself; do not merely look out for your own personal interests, but also for the interests of others" (Philippians 2:3–4, NASB). If each person in the relationship is striving to live out this verse, all needs will be met.

What happens when needs aren't met? Myron Rush says:

> Show me a person with hurting relationships and I'll show you a person with unfulfilled needs. You never destroy relationships by meeting too many of an individual's needs. However, failure to meet needs in a relationship is the fastest way I know to destroy it.
>
> An unfulfilled need has the same effect on your emotions as a misplaced hammer hit does on your finger—both get your undivided attention. Just as you feel the pain in your finger you feel the hurt and tension generated by an unfulfilled need.
>
> When our needs are not met we begin to focus on ourselves. We withdraw from those who refuse to meet our needs just like we avoid hitting our fingers again with the hammer. No one enjoys the hurt of unfulfilled needs; we do everything in our power to protect ourselves from such hurt. Our posture becomes extremely defensive and protective. Reluctant to run any risks in the relationship that might open up the wound, we spend more and more time avoiding the issues or people that have created the hurt.[3]

Unfortunately, there are some fearful, selfish, failing relationships in our lives which become destructive. Not only is the relationship no longer growing, but members are tearing each other down to the point of becoming depressed or demoralized. Adolescents experience destructive relationships quite frequently; but such also occur in the lives of adults.

There is a point at which destructive relationships will finally fall apart. I have seen them in my counseling office. I believe that marriages should stay together and attempt to work our their differences. But some marriages become very destructive. In the majority of divorce cases I know about the marriages were, in my estimation, salvageable if both partners had been willing to change and grow. But from time to time I encounter a marriage in which partners continue to destroy each other and their children through their selfishness. In such severe cases the relationship may need to end. I've also seen destructive relationships between fiancés and friends terminated or reduced to a lower level.

I like Leo Buscaglia's comment concerning the termination of a relationship: "We are not for everyone and everyone is not for us. The question is, 'If we cannot be with another, can we at least not hurt them? Can we, at least, find a way to coexist?'"[4] Diminishing or terminating a destructive relationship without hurting one another is an act of compassion and grace. Perhaps this is the real test of the presence of Jesus Christ in our lives to impact our relationships.

Three Vital Qualities for Getting Along

During more than twenty-five years as a professional counselor I have continued to study, learn, grow, and even change my ideas and approaches to people's problems. But while my counseling theories and styles have improved over the years, one ingredient has remained largely unchanged. I still believe that the three most vital qualities for getting along with people are *genuineness, nonpossessive love,* and *empathy.* These qualities were first suggested in the late 1950s and have been supported over more than three decades by about one hundred research studies.

When these three qualities are present, therapists develop constructive relationships with their patients, making progress possible. These qualities are present in teachers who foster the greatest student achievement. Physicians and nurses facilitate a patient's return to health by expressing these qualities as they apply their medical skills. Business leaders and managers reflecting these attitudes elicit greater motivation and less resistance in their employees. Salespersons with these qualities tend to have more satisfied customers. And these qualities are essential to productive courtship, marriage, and parenting.

Let's investigate more closely how the qualities of genuineness, nonpossessive love, and empathy can help you get along with almost anyone.

Genuineness. To get along with people, you must be genuine. This is the quality of being who you really are without a front or a facade. A genuine person is able to express his true feelings in appropriate ways, rather than suppress them or mask them. When a person is being genuine with you, as the saying goes, "What you see is what you get!"

Some people have a hard time being themselves. How tragic and how stressful to always be putting on an act. To be genuine, you need to know who you really are and accept that self-image. And when you always put up a false front before others, you may start to confuse your true identity with the "character" you are portraying. You may begin to wonder, *Who am I really?* That's one of the delights of being a Christian. We can accept who we are because of the way God sees us through His Son Jesus Christ.

Dale Carnegie once interviewed a magician named Howard Thurston who entertained more than sixty million people over his forty-year career. Carnegie asked Thurston why the magician had enjoyed such a successful career. Thurston admitted that many other magicians knew as much about the art as he did and were as gifted as he was. But he said he had two things the others did not. First, he was a master at timing and communication. He understood human nature and he was a real showman. Second, he was genuinely interested in people. He said that many magicians saw the audiences as a bunch of suckers or hicks. But every time Thurston went on stage, he said to himself, "I'm grateful because these people come to see me. They make it possible for me to make my living in a very enjoyable manner. I'm going to give them the best show I can possibly give them. I love these people."[5]

I wonder how many store employees say to themselves, "I'm grateful my customers come here to shop. I'm going to give them the best service possible." I wonder how many teachers say, "I'm glad my students are here today. I'm going to give them my best." It's rare to hear this kind of attitude today in our "me-first" society. But that's being genuine. People who express genuineness in this way get along with almost anyone.

A main ingredient in genuineness is sincerity. When someone is sincere, you can relax in the comfort and security that he or she is trustworthy. Sincerity also is a biblical quality. Paul prayed that the love of the Philippian believers would "abound still more and more in real knowledge and all discernment, so that you may approve the things that are excellent, in order to be sincere and blameless until the day of Christ" (Philippians 1:9–10, NASB).

Our word *sincere* comes from a Latin word which means "without wax." In ancient times, fine, expensive porcelain pottery often developed tiny cracks when it was fired in the kiln. Dishonest merchants would smear pearly white wax over the cracks until they disappeared, then claim the pottery was unblemished. But when the pottery was held up to the sun, the light would reveal the cracks filled in with wax. So honest merchants marked their porcelain with the words *sine cera*—without wax. That's what is meant by genuine sincerity: no hidden cracks, no ulterior motives, no hidden agendas.[6]

When Christ is in your life, it is so much easier to drop the facade and allow the genuine you to fully develop. But this genuineness develops over a period of time. The children's story, *The Velveteen Rabbit*, contains a delightful illustration of the way genuineness develops:

> "What is Real?" asked the Rabbit one day. "Does it mean having things that buzz inside you and a stick-out handle?"
> "Real isn't how you are made," said the Skin Horse. . . .
> "When a child loves you for a long, long time, not just to play with, but *really* loves you, then you become Real. It doesn't happen all at once," said the Skin Horse. "You become. It takes a long time. . . . Generally, by the time you are Real, most of your hair has been loved off and your eyes drop out and you get loose in the joints and very shabby. But these things don't matter at all, because once you are Real, you can't be ugly, except to people who don't understand."[7]

Being genuine with others involves another risky ingredient: transparency. Transparency, the ability to be seen for who you really are, is a rare commodity these days. It's easier and safer to wear a mask than to let others see who you are inside. But it's hard to build a relationship with someone wearing a mask. Jesus encouraged transparency when He said, "Blessed are the pure in heart, for they shall see God" (Matthew 5:8, NASB). The word *pure* literally means clean, uncontaminated, sincere, without corruption, alloy, or guile, and honest in motive. I enjoyed reading Chuck Swindoll's illustration of transparency:

> Last night I decided to try something I had never done before to drive home a point. At my last birthday my sister gave me a full-face rubber mask . . . one of those crazy things that slip over your entire head. She told me she'd give me ten dollars if I'd wear it into the pulpit one Sunday (my kids raised it to fifteen dollars), but I just couldn't do it! Well, last night I wore that ugly beast when I got up to speak. I figured if anybody could handle it, this gang could. *It was wild!*
>
> I didn't call attention to it. Without any explanation, I just stood up and began to speak on being authentic. There I stood pressing on, making one statement after another as the place came apart at the seams. Why? Anybody knows why! My mask canceled out everything I had to say, especially on *that* subject. It's impossible to be very convincing while you wear a mask.
>
> I finally pulled the thing off and the place settled down almost immediately. As soon as it did, everybody got the point. It's a funny thing, when we wear *literal* masks, nobody is fooled. But how easy it is to wear invisible ones and fake people out by the hundreds week after week. Did you know that the word *hypocrite* comes from the ancient Greek plays? An actor would place a large, grinning mask in front of his face and quote his comedy lines as the audience would roar with laughter. He would then slip backstage and grab a frowning, sad, oversized mask and come back quoting tragic lines as the audience would moan and weep. Guess what he was called. A *hypocritos,* one who wears a mask.
>
> Servants who are "pure in heart" have peeled off their masks. And God places a special blessing on their lives.[8]

Transparent people are remembered, appreciated, and trusted. Transparency is a health-insurance policy, because openness and honesty about who you are tends to prevent both mental illness and some kinds of physical illness.

Loy McGinnis tells the story of a famous psychiatrist who was leading a meeting on how to enable clients to become more open and transparent in their counseling sessions. He challenged his colleagues with a very strong statement: "I'll wager that my technique will enable me to get a new patient to talk about the most private things during the first session without my having to ask a question." What did he do? It was quite simple. He began the session by revealing to the client something personal about himself—a secret that could damage the psychiatrist if the client broke the confidence. The doctor's openness did the job. It freed the client to talk. And that's an important principle. We often sit around waiting for others to take the risk of opening up. But if we took the initiative to be transparent, the other person would be more likely to open up to us.[9]

Jesus was a transparent person. He lived among the disciples and repeatedly opened Himself up to them. When they misunderstood Him, He was grieved. He wanted them to understand what He was sharing with them, so one day He told them, "I no longer call you servants, because a servant does not know his master's business. Instead, I have called you friends, for everything that I learned from my Father I have made known to you" (John 15:15, NIV).

In a healthy relationship, individuals trust one another enough to become transparent and vulnerable. They feel secure to the extent that they believe the other person will not take advantage of them. There is no exploitation or taking one another for granted. Each can be open and honest without fear of being judged.

Who are the transparent people in your life? Toward whom are you transparent? I hope this quality is developing in your life and helping you to get along with others.

Nonpossessive love. The ability to love people nonpossessively is a second vital quality for getting along with others. Love draws people together. I'm not talking about emotional sentiment, but kindness, fairness, patience, and so many other characteristics of love from the Word of God.

Let's be brutally honest: There are some people you work with, go to church with, or are related to whom you don't like. Admit it; it's true! Yet the Bible tells us to love everyone. How can we reconcile these two realities? How can we love people we don't like? Our problem is we confuse love with an emotion. Love is not a feeling but an attitude and a willful act. To love someone means to wish for and work for that person's best interests, and to seek God's blessing upon him or her—whether or not we like that person! In fact, the unlikable, obnoxious, or impossible individuals are usually the ones who need our selfless, agape love the most.

A vivid illustration of nonpossessive love is found in Lorraine Hansberry's book, *Raisin in the Sun*. Walter, a grown son, squandered the family's money, forcing all the family to live in an undesirable environment. The family was furious with him. It seemed there really wasn't anything in Walter left to love. Walter's mother was quite hurt and disappointed, but she was wise enough to know that love can persist even when a person is unlikable. She reminds the family of this at a very tense moment:

> There is always something left to love. And if you ain't learned that, you ain't learned nothing. Have you cried for that boy today? I don't mean for yourself and for the family 'cause we lost the money. I mean for him; what he been through and what it done to him. Child, when do you think is the time to love somebody the most; when they done good and made things easy for everybody? Well then, you ain't through learning—because that ain't the time at all. It's when he's at his lowest and can't believe in hisself 'cause the world done whipped him so. When you starts measuring somebody, measure him right, child, measure him right. Make sure you done taken into account what hills and valleys he come through before he got to wherever he is.[10]

When you love someone, you accept that person—even if he or she is a prodigal like Walter. You are uncontaminated by negative evaluations of that person's thoughts, feelings, or behaviors. It doesn't mean you necessarily approve of his behavior. You can be accepting and confronting at the same time—accepting the person and confronting his or her behavior. But the emphasis is on learning to get along with that person by expressing nonpossessive, "in-spite-of" love.

Empathy. The third vital quality for getting along with people is empathy. Perhaps the best way to define this quality is to describe it with actual examples.

About two centuries ago, John Woolman was a living example of empathy. He walked barefooted from Baltimore to Philadelphia to experience personally some of the pain suffered by the black slaves who were forced to walk barefooted over great distances. By going through this experience he understood better what the slaves experienced.

Years ago in Cleveland, an executive in a major steel company resigned his position and took a job as a common laborer in another city. As he worked side by side with other laborers, he developed a new perspective on the problems laborers experienced. His empathetic endeavor led him into the field of labor relations and he became a recognized authority in that area.

Empathy comes from the German word *einfulung*, which means to feel into or to feel with. Empathy is viewing life through another's eyes, feeling as another feels, hearing the story through the perceptions of the other person. Christians are called to empathy by bearing one another's burdens (Galatians 6:2) and by rejoicing with others in their joys and weeping with others in their pain (Romans 12:15).

Some people confuse empathy with apathy and sympathy, which sound similar but actually are quite different. Sympathy means you are overinvolved in the emotions of others. Sympathy can actually undermine your emotional strength so that you are incapable of helping when you are most needed. Apathy means you are uninvolved with others. Empathy means walking with another person in his inner world.

Apathy has *no* feelings for another; sympathy is feeling *for* another; and empathy is feeling *with* another. Apathy says, "I don't care"; sympathy says, "Oh, you poor thing"; and empathy says, "It looks like you're having a difficult time today."

We must try to see through the eyes of others how their world appears to them. Empathy sees another's joys, perceives what underlies those joys, and communicates this understanding to the person. When someone has empathy for us, we experience the satisfaction of being understood and accepted because another person sees our point of view. That's the kind of satisfaction we can give to others as we express empathy to them.[11]

What do you have to offer others? Why do I ask such a question? Because what you offer the people you're trying to get along with is often what they will offer you in return. If you offer anger, you are likely to receive anger in return. If you offer criticism, you will be criticized in return. But if you offer concern, compassion, respect, and love, you will probably be on the receiving end of those qualities as well.

Have you ever tried the sidewalk test? When you walk down a crowded sidewalk, purposely frown at several people coming from the other direction. Don't be surprised if people frown back at you or even turn away. Then greet several people with a friendly smile. Most people will respond in a similar manner, and some may even be encouraged to speak a friendly word to you.

When you get into a crowded elevator and begin to complain about the wait, the crowds, the rain, or the heat, you will find others joining you in your grumpy, complaining mood. But if you crack a joke, express some humor about the bad weather, or point out something positive, others will respond in a positive vein. Did you realize how much influence you can have on others? It's amazing! You really have the power to get along with almost anyone. It may take some adjustments on your part, but you *can* do it.

2

Job One: Getting Along with Number One

Jim had been coming in for counseling for about six months. Each week we ended up talking about his basic problem: people. Jim didn't get along with his family, his co-workers, or people in general. We seemed to be getting nowhere in counseling until, during one counseling session, Jim made an amazing discovery seemingly by accident. He said, almost in a joking manner, "Norm, at times I wonder if my problem of getting along with other people is really a problem of getting along with myself." Jim was right. He wasn't much of a friend to others because he wasn't much of a friend to himself. He had stumbled onto a foundational principle for interpersonal relationships: You can't get along with others if you have difficulty getting along with yourself. The way you treat others will reflect the way you treat yourself.

A friend is someone you treat with high regard. You like his qualities, accept his strengths and weaknesses, and enjoy being with him. But are you a friend to yourself? Do you delight in your positive qualities, accept your negative qualities, and generally enjoy being yourself? I'm not talking about the conceit of looking out for Number One at all costs, pushing yourself forward, or tooting your own horn. I'm referring to the healthy self-acceptance which is suggested in Jesus' words, "Love your neighbor as yourself" (Matthew 22:39, NIV). Before you can lovingly get along with others as Christ commanded, you must learn to accept and love yourself.

Give Yourself a Break

We've all heard people exclaim in frustration, "Give me a break!" They're usually expressing a sense of being overwhelmed and pressured by their circumstances. They feel like the world is closing in on them. Do you ever say that to yourself? Do you ever put so much pressure on yourself or come down so hard on yourself that you cry out, "Give me a break!"? Are your expectations for yourself sometimes so high that you are overly critical of yourself? I'm guilty of that. Sometimes I expect too much of myself by attempting too many tasks at once or overloading my time schedule. We don't realize that the unfair pressure we exert on ourselves will eventually be reflected in the unfair pressure we place on the people we are trying to get along with.

I much prefer the advertising slogan of several years ago, "You deserve a break today." That's what you ought to be saying when you are tempted to be too hard on yourself. The Word of God tells us to be kind to one another. But are you kind to yourself? And what about other biblical qualities we are to express toward people—grace, love, forgiveness, patience, and so on? Do you apply these qualities to yourself? The only way you can truly express these qualities to others is through learning to express them to yourself first.

We deserve the break of accepting ourselves for who we are, imperfections and all. Self-acceptance hasn't always been easy for me. Sometimes I'm pretty tough on myself. Do you know what has helped me the most in this area? It's knowing that God loves me for who I am. His acceptance is my source of security and comfort. And He loves and accepts you, too. The extent of His great love is seen in His willingness to adopt us as His own children (see John 1:12 and 1 John 3:1). If God can accept us as we are, why shouldn't we do the same? I'm always encouraged in this area by the words of J.I. Packer in his book, *Knowing God:*

There is tremendous relief in knowing that His love to me is utterly realistic, based at every point on prior knowledge of the worst about me, so that no discovery now can disillusion Him about me, in the way I am so often disillusioned about myself, and quench His determination to bless me. There is, certainly, great cause for humility in the thought that He sees all the twisted things about me that my fellow men do not see (and I am glad!), and that He sees more corruption in me than . . . I see in myself. There is, however, equally great incentive to worship and love God in the thought that, for some unfathomable reason He wants me as His friend, and desires to be my friend, and has given His Son to die for me in order to realize this purpose.[1]

Knowing that God loves and accepts us is the key to a healthy self-image. But many people are confused by terms like self-image, self-esteem, self-love, self-surrender, self-crucifixion, self-denial, and self-respect. Humility and pride seem to be all mixed together. In his outstanding book, *Healing Grace,* David Seamands calls it "a tangled mess." Yet the Scriptures clearly infer that a proper self-love constitutes the basis for relating to others (see Leviticus 19:18,34; Matthew 19:19; 22:39; Luke 10:27; Romans 13:9; Galatians 5:14; James 2:8). Seamands shares the following insights:

The Scriptures *everywhere* assume that an appropriate self-love, self-care, and self-appreciation is normal, and *nowhere* tell us to hate or neglect ourselves, or to indulge in self-depreciation.

Self-denial consists in denying not our self-worth but our self-will, and in abandoning our search for self-glory. The crucifixion of the self is our willingness to renounce our carnal, self-glorifying self and allow it to be put to death on the cross with Christ. It does not mean we renounce or belittle our God-given gifts; it does mean we surrender them to God to be used for His glory. Pride, as it is used in the Bible, is a dishonest estimate of ourselves. Paul warns against this: "For by the grace given to me I say to every one of you, Do not think of yourself more highly than you ought, but rather think of yourself with sober judgment, in accordance with the measure of faith God has given you" (Romans 12:3). Just as Paul reminds us we are saved by grace through faith and that not of ourselves, he here reminds us that God's grace and our faith will also give us an honest and accurate estimate of ourselves.[2]

Make Room for Your Weak Spots

In Greek mythology, Achilles was a great warrior. His mother dipped him into the river Styx as an infant to make him invulnerable to attack. The magical waters of the river covered everything except Achilles' heel, by which his mother held him. As he grew to manhood, Achilles conquered all his foes. He was invincible in the Trojan War until his enemy Paris struck him with a fatal arrow in his only vulnerable spot, his heel.

All of us have Achilles heels. They are our weak spots, the vulnerable areas of our lives. We can learn from our weaknesses and allow them to challenge us to grow and improve. But too often people ignore their weaknesses and allow them to spread to other areas of their lives. Other people ignore their strengths and see only their weaknesses. By focusing on their Achilles heels, they give their weaknesses greater influence in their lives.

We should neither ignore nor accentuate our weaknesses. Either extreme will negatively affect self-image. Getting along with yourself involves identifying and facing both your strengths and your weaknesses as an individual.

The following exercise will help you learn more about how you view yourself. Complete each "except for" and "if only" statement to help you identify your Achilles heels. Then share your responses with a trusted friend or relative and ask for their feedback on your observations.

I usually feel good about myself except for . . .
I feel good about my body and appearance except for . . .
I am generally in control of my life except for . . .
I am usually in control of my emotions except for . . .
I get along with people most of the time except for . . .
I believe other people see me as an okay person except for . . .
I usually make good decisions and choices in life except for . . .

When I look in the mirror, I feel satisfied with myself
except for . . .
    I would be more satisfied with my life if only . . .
    My family would be more satisfied with me if only . . .
    My marriage or family relationships would be more sat-
isfying to me if only . . .
    I could accept myself better if only . . .
    I could get along with others better if only . . .
    I could reach out more to other people if only . . .
    I could overcome my weaknesses if only . . .

What did you learn about yourself? Did you discover
your Achilles heel? Do your answers indicate that you are a
friend to yourself despite your weaknesses?

Dr. Harold Bloomfield has been helping clients and seminar participants deal with their weaknesses for more than
fifteen years. He asks them, "What is your Achilles' heel?"
The responses he has received fall into five major categories:
(1) I'm afraid of getting hurt again; (2) When I look in the
mirror, I'm never quite satisfied; (3) I can't stand criticism;
(4) I'm always feeling tense and rushed; (5) I wish I could be
happier.[3] How do these statements match up with your responses?

Do you realize that the Achilles tendon in the heel is
only about three inches long? And yet an injury to that tiny
spot can completely immobilize a basketball star who is
seven feet tall! Similarly, many of us allow relatively insignif-
icant weaknesses to dominate our lives while neglecting our
more obvious strengths and spiritual gifts. One woman I
counseled told me that her large nose completely ruined her
appearance. Another woman said she was rejected by a boy
when she was seventeen and she has been looking for the
defect he saw in her ever since, still unable to trust men. A
forty-year-old man admitted to me that he made a small mistake at work three years earlier and has seen himself as a
total failure since the incident.

We must learn to keep our weaknesses in proper propor-
tion. A recent client came for counseling saying, "Norm, let
me tell you about myself. Here are my strengths," and he
listed them for me. Then he itemized his weaknesses, adding,
"I'm working hard to change the first three. But I doubt if I

will be able to do much about the other two since they involve natural ability. But I will continue to participate in those areas since I enjoy the activity."

I soon realized that the man talking to me was a balanced person. He did not define himself by his weaknesses, but kept them in proper perspective. He appreciated himself as he was, accepting and dealing with his weaknesses as part of the total package. I wish more people would learn to do this.

Life without Regrets

I have talked with a number of individuals who keep an extensive list of regrets concerning their lives. For many of them, their present lives seem to be overshadowed by the weaknesses and failures of the past. Some of our regrets are deeply imbedded in the subconscious and inaccessible. But most of them are close enough to the surface that we are aware of them and feel their impact. Holding onto regrets is like celebrating the anniversaries of failures—except feelings of regret usually come around more often than once a year. We spend so much emotional time and energy commemorating these negative events from the past that we have trouble getting along with ourselves and others in the present.

Overcoming personal regrets is an important step in learning to get along with yourself and others. The process of overcoming regrets is modeled after the process by which war veterans, policemen, firemen, and other victims of traumatic experiences overcome their painful memories. The first step is to list the regrets of your life. For example, here is a list compiled by a forty-five-year-old man:

I regret that I never spent enough time with my son before he left home.

I regret my hesitation in speaking up more when I had feelings and insights.

I regret being so busy with work that I missed out on my children's activities.

I regret that I let my fears control my life and limit my productivity.

I regret that I haven't told my wife how much I care for her.

I regret the times I have lied to get out of difficult situations.

The second step is to list the ways your regrets have influenced your life. Then describe in writing what you think your life could be like if these memories were no longer regrets, but only historical facts which no longer affect you. Before reading on, take a moment to complete these first two steps on a blank sheet of paper.

The third step is to give your regrets to Jesus Christ. If your regret involves a sinful act from the past, accept His forgiveness and forgive yourself. Remember the assuring words of Charles Wesley's hymn, "He breaks the power of cancelled sin, He sets the prisoner free." If your regret is a failure instead of a sin, tell yourself that you don't need to be dominated by the past. Even though you wish you would have acted differently then, decide to go on with your life free from the effects of your failure. If your regret involves behaviors or responses you can change, write down your plan for change.

As you complete this exercise, praise God for your freedom from personal regrets. Praise is a healing balm for painful regrets and "if onlys." The God you praise will provide all the strength you need for living beyond your regrets. Lloyd Ogilvie wrote:

> Praising the Lord makes us willing and releases our imaginations to be used by Him to form the picture of what He is seeking to accomplish. A resistant will makes us very uncreative and lacking in adventuresome vision in the use of our capacity of imagination. God wants to use our imagination in the painting of the picture of what He is leading us to dare to hope for and expect. We become what we envision under *the Spirit's guidance.* That's why our own image of ourselves, other people, our goals, and our projects all need the inspiration of our imagination. However, until the Holy Spirit begins His work releasing it, our will keeps our imagination stunted and immature.[4]

Beware of Roadblocks

Numerous hindrances prevent us from getting along with ourselves. But two of them are the most common and debilitating. The good news is that both of these roadblocks can be eliminated.

Fear. Some people are so driven by fear that they are crippled in their endeavors to accept themselves and relate to others. Fear freezes and paralyzes people, preventing them from getting the most out of life. Fear keeps people from making the necessary changes which will allow them to relate better to others.

Many people I talk to are afraid of death; but even more are afraid of life. Experiencing the full potential of life is a threat to them. They are emotionally paralyzed and they refuse to participate in many of life's normal experiences and relationships. They are afraid of being hurt, being rejected, making a mistake, showing their imperfections, and failing as persons. Fear causes people to avoid taking risks and being vulnerable. They become turtles who live inside a defensive shell of fear, immobile and detached from life.

Fear is a powerful *negative* drive. It compels you forward and inhibits your progress at the same time. Fear is like a noose that slowly tightens around your neck if you move in the wrong direction. Those who are afraid of what other people think of them seem to walk on eggshells. By overemphasizing the responses of others, they wrongly give others the power to determine their worth. An overconcern with the responses of others reflects a person's failing struggle to get along with himself.

Fear is also like a videotape which continually replays our most haunting experiences, embarrassing moments, rejections, failures, hurts, and disappointments. These instant replays cause a person to say, "I can't do it; I may fail." Have you ever said to yourself, "I'll never be able to get along with those people. I'll never be able to get along with myself. I'll never like myself or accept myself"? If so, you've been watching too many horror films from your past.[5]

The antidote for fear is hope. Hope is a powerful *positive* drive, a motivating force which can change your life. It can change how you get along with yourself and others. It is like a magnet that draws you toward your goal. Hope is like a videotape continually replaying scenes of opportunity, change, and potential for you and your relationships. And the sound track on that tape is God's message of hope to us: "You can do it. Trust in Me and allow Me to free you from your prison of fears."

Which videotape are you watching—fear or hope? Are you hopeful about yourself? Are you hopeful about your relationships with people who are difficult to get along with? You can be. Take for yourself the hope Paul wrote about: "For God did not give us a spirit of timidity, but a spirit of power, of love an of self-discipline" (2 Timothy 1:7, NIV).

Perfectionism. A second formidable roadblock to getting along with ourselves is the attitude of perfectionism. A perfectionist strives to be complete and flawless in all respects of his life. He thinks, *If I make no mistakes, I cannot criticize myself or be criticized by others. If I'm perfect in every way, I can accept myself and I will get along with others all the time.*

I have never met a successful perfectionist—and neither have you—because it's impossible for anyone to be perfect. Perfectionism is a figment of the imagination. And yet the attitude of perfectionism, like its close cousin, fear, often dominates people's lives. Would-be perfectionists have difficulty getting along with themselves because they continually fail to meet their own unrealistic, uncompromising standards and expectations. Even when a task is 90 percent successful, the perfectionist considers it a total failure because it wasn't 100 percent successful.

Because of the constant frustration of not being perfect, perfectionists are often angry people. They cannot accept themselves because they are continually less than acceptable in their performance. They are also the perpetual, unforgiving critics of everyone else for their imperfections. If you are hounded by a perfectionistic attitude, you'll have trouble getting along with yourself and everybody else.

God didn't call us to live perfect lives, but He did call us to grow, improve, develop, and work toward a standard of excellence. Excellence is that which is outstandingly good or of exceptional merit. Though we are imperfect, all of us have the potential to achieve excellence in some areas of our lives while accepting our weaknesses in others. For example, even though I am constantly learning and growing as a professional counselor, I have realized a certain amount of success in this field. In contrast, I have learned to accept the fact that I will never achieve excellence working with my hands. As a junior-high student, I worked for three weeks in woodworking class building a toy sailboat. When I showed it to the teacher, he said, "Norm, I'm glad you told me what it is. Have you ever thought about transferring to typing class?" And recently I confirmed my nickname "Three Thumbs" by trying, failing, and then finally succeeding to assemble a new "easy-to-assemble" bookshelf.

When you work toward excellence, you do what you do to the best of your ability. You leave room in your life for growth, forgiving yourself for your shortcomings and imperfections. When you struggle in one area, you think about your strengths and successes in other areas. And you remain flexible, because flexible people have the best opportunity to get along with almost everyone—including themselves.[6] We will look at the importance of flexibility in chapter seven.

Freedom to Fail

How do you feel when you make a mistake or when you're wrong? Terrible? Horrible? Totally depressed? Many people feel this way; but others learn to accept the imperfections of their humanity. To get along with yourself, you need to handle your mistakes in a positive way.

I'm intrigued by the following statements which highlight the positive side of making mistakes:

Why It's Great to Make Mistakes

1. I fear making mistakes because I see everything in absolutist, perfectionistic terms—one mistake and the whole is ruined. This is erroneous. A small mistake certainly doesn't ruin an otherwise fine whole.

2. It's good to make mistakes because then we learn— in fact, we won't learn unless we make mistakes. No one can avoid making mistakes—and since it's going to happen in any case, we may as well accept it and learn from it.

3. Recognizing our mistakes helps us to adjust our behavior so that we can get results we're more pleased with—

so we might say that mistakes ultimately operate to make us happier and make things better.

4. If we fear mistakes, we become paralyzed—we're afraid to do or try anything, since we might (in fact, probably will) make some mistakes. If we restrict our activities so that we won't make mistakes, then we are really defeating ourselves. The more we try and the more mistakes we make, the faster we'll learn and the happier we'll be ultimately.

5. Most people aren't going to be mad at us or dislike us because we make mistakes—they all make mistakes and most people feel uncomfortable around "perfect" people.

6. We don't die if we make mistakes.[7]

When singer Marian Anderson was just getting started, the members of her church in Philadelphia collected pennies, nickels, and dimes to help her get to New York for her singing debut at Town Hall. But Marian lacked maturity and experience, and the critics massacred her. She returned to Philadelphia in disgrace and could not bring herself to face her friends. Her depression lasted for more than a year.

But Marian Anderson's mother would not give up on her. "Failure is only temporary, Marian," she said. "Grace must come before greatness. Why don't you think about failure a little and pray about it a lot?"

Marian Anderson followed her mother's advice and went on to become a great singer. In turn, she has encouraged other struggling performers through their times of failure and despair.

Charles Knight, the chief executive officer of Emerson Electric, was asked to comment on the ingredients of good management. He said, "You need the ability to fail. I'm amazed at the number of organizations that set up an environment where they do not permit their people to be wrong. You cannot innovate unless you are willing to accept some mistakes."[8]

Some people think failure is fatal. That's a myth. Failure, and the ability to learn from failure, make for lasting success.

The Critic Within

If you're like most of us, you started adult life with very little. You moved into your first apartment with hand-me-down furniture, appliances, and utensils donated by relatives and friends. Some of those furnishings weren't in very nice condition, and there were days when you wanted to toss everything out. But you couldn't afford to fill an entire apartment with new furnishings, and it was uncomfortable sitting, eating, and sleeping on the floor. So you kept the sagging couch, the broken chairs, and chipped dishes until you could replace them a piece at a time.

Your mind is kind of like that apartment. As a young adult, many of your thoughts and ideas about yourself were hand-me-downs from your parents, friends, teachers, and others who influenced you while you were growing up. Some of those thoughts may have been negative, critical, and even sinful. As you have grown older these thoughts have hindered you from maintaining a good self-image and getting along with yourself. But you can't just empty your mind of negative thoughts. You cannot live in a mental vacuum. You must replace old, negative, critical hand-me-down thoughts with positive biblical thoughts.

Herman Gockel makes an interesting statement about the empty mind:

> There is much more to this whole business than merely getting rid of negative or unworthy thoughts. In fact, the concept of "getting rid" is itself a sign of negative thinking. We shall succeed in this whole matter, not in the measure in which we empty our minds of sinful and degrading thoughts, but rather in the measure in which we *fill* them with thoughts that are wholesome and uplifting. The human mind can never be a vacuum. He who thinks he can improve the tenants of his soul simply by evicting those that are unworthy will find that for every unworthy tenant he evicts through the back door several more will enter through the front (see Matthew 12:43–45). It is not merely a matter of evicting. It is also a matter of screening, selecting, admitting, and cultivating those tenants that have proved themselves desirable.[9]

What do you say to yourself about yourself? Your inner thoughts about yourself reflect your self-esteem. Over the years I've heard many people make statements such as these which revealed how they were getting along (or not getting along!) with themselves:

When will I learn to do it right?
I can't get my life together.
I'm not a creative person.
I just know that today is going to turn out rotten!
I just freeze up in new situations.
I'm really out of shape.
Boy, is that going to be hard for me to do!
Every time I lose weight, it hides around the corner and then jumps right back on.
I can't trust him anymore.
If only I had the breaks he's had.

Negative statements like these get results—but not the kind you want! They are self-fulfilling prophecies: The more you say them to yourself, the more they come true. For example, when you say, "This is going to be difficult," you are setting yourself up for a difficult time. Even if the possibility of difficulties is great for my counselees, I encourage them to say, "This is going to be difficult, but I can learn to do it." It helps turn a negative thought into a realistic, positive statement.

We also have a hard time getting along with ourselves when we talk to ourselves in negative, critical terms. It's like living with a critical person all the time—and the critic lives inside you! This internal critic continually berates you, inspecting your thoughts and actions with a magnifying glass that enlarges minor perfections into major problems. When you were a child, you were taught not to talk back to the authority figures who criticized and corrected you. But if you still have an authoritarian critic browbeating you from within, it's time to speak up and put it in its place—which is not inside you.

If you battle self-criticism, it is probably because you suffer from feelings of insecurity. Often the anxiety connected with doubting your acceptance by others will cause you to strive to reach the ideals those others hold for you. To please others, you place excessively high standards on yourself. You may look successful on the outside, but inside you can't quite measure up to those unrealistic ideals—and your internal critic never lets you forget it. Others may applaud the facade they see, but inside you think, *If they only knew.* The real you doesn't have a chance to emerge because of the pressure of keeping up the facade. Some call this the impostor complex— pretending to be one thing while battling the fear that others will discover who you really are. As long as you are fighting this battle fueled by negative, critical thoughts and feelings, you will have trouble connecting with other people.[10]

Let's take a practical approach to dealing with the critical tenant in your mind. Create a personal eviction notice for your negative thoughts and replace them with positive thoughts. Divide a blank sheet of paper into two columns. In the column on the left, write down some (at least three, but no more than fifteen) critical or negative comments that you tend to make to yourself. In the column on the right, rewrite each negative comment into a positive statement and explain what you intend to do to fulfill that statement. Don't overstate or understate your capabilities here; be honest about what you can and cannot do. For example, if you criticize yourself for not being able to carry a tune, don't state that you are going to become a great singer. Simply state that it's okay to be nonmusical and that you accept your inability to sing.

Here's an example:

Critical Tenant	. . . Positive Tenant
I can't get ahead in my work, I don't have the ability.	I do have some capabilities. If my abilities don't fit in this position, I can look into another position. I can also try some vocational testing. I am not deficient.
The pressure of this job and my family is too much. I can't handle it.	I've handled pressure in the past. I have more resources than I am giving myself credit for. I will share with my family how I am feeling and enlist their help.
Sometimes I wish I were someone else. I have so many personal faults.	I have much to offer to myself and others. I'm a good listener and I'm kind. It's true that I'm going bald, but that isn't a defect. It's part of growing older. It's what God has designed. I will give myself three positive affirmations each morning.

The next step is to make a list of past personal achievements you feel good about. In what activities did you succeed? At what times were you down on yourself, but then encouraged yourself?

As you think about displacing your negative self-talk with positive statements and actions, answer these questions: With whom have you shared your feelings? How would you like someone else to help you in this process? How can you benefit from others who have felt the same way? How will you call upon the power and strength of God to help you at this time? What scriptures will encourage you at this time?

Seeing Is Believing

If you want to learn to get along with yourself, you need to believe that it can happen. The key to change is *believing* in change. Believe in the power and presence of Jesus Christ to assist you in overcoming your self-doubts. See yourself developing your potential the way God sees you. How can you do this? Consider Chuck Swindoll's suggestion:

> Perhaps the best single-word picture is visualize. Those who break through the "mediocrity barrier," mentally visualize being on a higher plane. Then once they "see it," they begin to believe it and behave like it. People who soar are those who refuse to sit back, sigh, and wish things would change. They neither complain of their lot nor passively dream of some distant ship coming in. Rather, they visualize in their minds that they are not quitters; they will not allow life's circumstances to push them down and hold them under.[11]

Imagination is the creative function within us. It's the way we see things. For change and growth to occur, a person must both creatively imagine and specifically define what he wants. The main element involved in this process of changing our thoughts is encountering the Word of God in a radical, new way. For some, the words of Scripture are not new; for others, they may be. But knowing God's Word and practicing it are two different things. Chuck Swindoll says:

In order for old defeating thoughts to be invaded, conquered, and replaced by new, victorious ones, a process of reconstruction must transpire. The best place I know to begin this process of mental cleansing is with the all-important discipline of memorizing Scripture. I realize it doesn't sound very sophisticated or intellectual, but God's Book is full of powerful ammunition. And dislodging negative and demoralizing thoughts requires aggressive action.[12]

Become your own cheerleader. Encourage yourself. Have faith in who you are, not just in what you can do. God's Word describes the result of our negative messages to ourselves: "Death and life are in the power of the tongue, and they who indulge it shall eat the fruit of it [for death or life]" (Proverbs 18:21, AMP). That verse is not only true for how you respond to others, but also for how you talk to yourself. Paul says, "Therefore encourage one another and build each other up" (1 Thessalonians 5:11, NIV). We need to encourage ourselves in order to be able to encourage others.

Jesus Christ wants us to have a realistic, honest perspective of who we are. He wants us to bring the negative untruths about ourselves to Him, and He wants us to direct our thoughts toward all we can be under His guidance. Invite Jesus to be the primary tenant of your mind, going from room to room, cleaning out the old and bringing in the new. As you do this, you will be able to greet yourself and say with all honesty, "I'm glad to meet you. You are someone worth knowing." As we learn to get along with ourselves in this way, we can turn our attention to learning to get along with almost anyone.

If you are interested in reading more on the subjects discussed in this chapter, I recommend these resources: *Living with a Perfectionist,* by David Stoop; *Healing Grace,* by David Seamands; *Uncovering Your Hidden Fears,* by Norman Wright; and *Making Peace with Your Past,* by Norman Wright.

3

Change Starts Where the Buck Stops

Sam made an appointment for counseling and was very prompt for his first session. He said, "Norm, I'm here because I have a few people at my place of business who are very difficult to get along with. They're problem people—which I refer to as PPs—and we're devoting far too much time to them in our office. If we could just get them to change their behavior and not be so much of a problem to everyone, our production would increase and we could eliminate a lot of difficulties in the office."

After listening to Sam vividly describe his problem for about five minutes, I asked, "Sam, are you also saying that you have difficulty getting along with some of these people?"

"At times it's difficult for me," he admitted. "But some of my co-workers have a much greater problem dealing with them than I do. And some of my friends at work need some help in learning how to deal with the PPs. But my main reason for coming to see you is for you to help me figure out a way to change these PPs. I'm sure there must be a way."

Does Sam's problem sound familiar? There are times in our lives when we've said, "If only so-and-so would change, everything would be so much better!"

After Sam had thoroughly presented his situation, it was time to begin working on a solution: "Sam, there are three possible ways to resolve this problem," I told him. "If it's okay with you, I would like to explore all three of those ways with you." Sam eagerly agreed.

"One way to rid your company of problem people is to change the environment. In this instance, it may involve transferring those people to another office or division. If they are a real serious problem, you might consider replacing them. What do you think of this option?"

Sam responded immediately. "I don't think that would work. There are too many problems and unpleasant consequences with reassigning people. Give me another option."

I said, "Here's another approach: Have you ever tried to change the way the problem people are themselves—the way they respond at work? Have you talked to them, made suggestions, considered options, encouraged them, complimented them, affirmed them—"

Sam interrupted me. "Norm, I think I've tried everything that you've suggested. Perhaps I haven't done very much with compliments and encouragement. When the PPs create so many problems, it's difficult to do that. No, the direct approach hasn't worked very well. I'm hoping that you have another sure-fire tactic or method which would do the trick."

"There is one other possibility that you could try," I responded, "and it's always had the best results of any approach." Then I paused, looking at Sam with a smile on my face, waiting to see if he could figure it out first.

Suddenly Sam's expression turned to pain. "Oh no, Norm! You're not going to suggest that old line, 'If you want someone to change, start by changing yourself,' are you?"

"Do you have a better idea, Sam? You said that what you have already tried hasn't worked. This is the best way I've found."

Sam's reply was characteristic of how many people feel about making changes in their lives: "I don't think it's fair that I have to change. After all, the PPs are the problem. Why shouldn't they change?"

"That may be true, Sam," I agreed. "But can you suggest another way to change them?"

Sam was thoughtfully silent for a moment. Then he said, "What should I change and how should I go about it? It's not easy, you know. These people do and say things which really push my buttons. I just want to put them in their places and get on with life."

"Sam, you're telling me that you allow the problem people to control you. You're saying that when they do or say certain things, you can't control yourself. How long have these people had this much control over you?"

Sam's face looked pale from shock. He almost shouted out his response, "You're right! I've been so dumb! I never saw it before! I've been letting them determine how I act. To be honest, I'm not real proud of how I've acted sometimes. I've let them push my buttons and blamed them for the trouble which resulted. But I guess I've really cooperated with them, haven't I?" Sam said it so well. We often allow others to get to us without seeing how we cooperate with them through our reactions.

Start with Yourself

To get along in relationships where changes are necessary, you need to start by changing yourself. Changing yourself just works better than trying to change others. And even if you see no changes in other people, your own changes will make life better for you and will reflect God's Word and power in your life. When you change, your bad relationships can turn to good relationships, and your good relationships can get even better.

If someone around me is grumpy and snaps at me, I may feel like snapping back. Our typical response to an attack is either to become defensive or to counterattack. But why should I let another's behavior dictate the way I behave? If someone is having a bad day, he or she doesn't need further negative input from me. What is needed is a kind word, a smile, an empathetic comment, or an offer of help. The change needs to start with me. It's amazing what can happen when we respond to negative people in a kind, loving, positive way.

The desire to see changes occur in relationships, and to pursue those changes, is normal. When we care about others and are committed to relationships with them, the desire for positive change in their lives is healthy. Without this kind of commitment to bring out the best in each other, we don't have much of a relationship.

But problems can arise when our desire for change in the other person exceeds our willingness to change ourselves. This attitude is apparent when the focus of change becomes "you" instead of "me." Also, trouble is inevitable when our request for change ("You might consider . . .") in someone else escalates to a demand ("You must . . ."). Yes, there are some people who are unpleasant to be around and difficult to get along with. True, there are occasions when the other person *is* the major problem in the relationship. But regardless of how much he or she may be at fault, the most direct route to a change in someone else is to make the necessary changes in yourself.

Changing vs. Coping

Time after time, people have complained to me during counseling, "There is no way that person"—a spouse, boss, co-worker, parent, in-law, etc.—"is going to change. Norm, you must teach me how to cope with him." The word "cope" bothers me. It suggests a passive approach to problem people. Too often coping leads to one of four unhealthy responses:

Resignation. Over the years I have hired a number of people in our organization. From time to time, one will resign from the staff and move on to new employment. Often it is a move to a better job or a different city. Sometimes a woman in the office resigns to start her career at home as a mother. These kinds of resignations are positive.

But resignation in a relationship is almost always negative, especially resigning one to the belief that the other person will never change. This person throws up the hands and cries out, "I give up! My attempts to bring about change haven't worked." Resignation admits defeat, communicating that a change will never happen, so we might as well accept the problem and learn to live with it. Resignation reflects a feeling of impotence in the relationship. A relationship in which one or more partners resign is in grave danger.

When we accept the belief that another person cannot change, we are not seeing that individual as God sees him or her. We must cling to the belief that others can change. We may not be involved in the process of change in that person; we may not be the agents of change God chooses to use. But when we resign all hope and expectations of change, we're not giving God much room to work. After all, it may be the wrong time for a change, or our approach may be the wrong approach. But that doesn't mean change will never happen at some other time and through some other means.

Resignation is an attitude which prompts one to deny other people permission to be the way they are because one doesn't like them that way. But there are some behaviors in others which we can permit for the time being, realizing that God can change that behavior in His own time. When you resign to living with a person whose offensive behavior you believe will not change, you are one step closer to learning to live without that person. In a marriage relationship, such a step is dangerous and scary. The feeling of impotence in the relationship can have a deteriorating effect upon your self-esteem, and you may project this view onto your partner. You begin to think less of him or her. Caring and commitment diminish, and you begin to withdraw permanently. Separation and divorce are just around the corner.

Instead of resigning to a relationship where change seems impossible, I prefer the term *positive acceptance*. Positive acceptance means that we say to the other person, "I accept you for who you are and how you respond. I still love you through the love of Christ. I will learn to respond to you in a new and healthy manner, and I will also move ahead in my own life. I would like you to change, but I probably will not be involved in the process."

Martyrdom. Another unhealthy response coping may produce, especially in close relationships, is martyrdom. This response to a changeless spouse or close friend says, "Staying with you will probably ruin me, but I guess it's the cross I must bear." Martyred individuals resort either to silently complaining to themselves or outwardly complaining to others to elicit sympathy for their sad lot in life. But in time the others turn deaf ears to these whining complaints, so the martyrdom is made worse by rejection. As with resignation, martyrdom leads to distancing in relationships since both caring and commitment erode between the martyrs and their unchanging partners.

These first two coping responses are fairly passive. Let's look now at a couple of more active negative responses.

Revenge. The vengeful cry of those who feel trapped in relationships they cannot change is, "Let's get them!" I have seen revenge at work in companies, church staffs, families, and other groups. Revenge does little to help us get along with others or build relationships. It is an action *against* others, not *for* them. Since revenge is anti-people, it is also anti-relationships.

Withdrawal. This is the most direct, dramatic, and devastating approach to relationships we cannot change. Withdrawal says, "If I can't change you, then I refuse to be involved with you." The relationship is terminated by one or more members, even though they may still remain in physical proximity. Withdrawal is present in many families today where the members are connected only by their blood ties. It is present in the work environment where people work together in polite toleration of each other, but have no relationship. There are other situations where withdrawal includes a painful, total, physical separation. Total physical withdrawal is the most common response in a relationship where one partner completely refuses to change. Total withdrawal may be the healthiest response if a continuation of the relationship promises to be destructive.[1]

Nobody Likes to Change

If you are attempting to improve a relationship and develop a greater level of peace and harmony with another person, and you are trying to change that person in the process, expect the inevitable: resistance! If you say, "I want you to change to improve our relationship," the other person will probably counter with, "I don't want to change." The resistance may not be this blatant and obvious, but it will rear its ugly head. The following five responses are among the most common tactics of resistance used by people when challenged to change:

1. "Oh, I'm sorry. I wasn't listening." This person doesn't really listen since he or she doesn't have any intention of changing.
2. "Oh, sure, I'll take care of it right away." This person may talk about changing, but for some reason he or she never gets around to doing it.
3. "How can you say such a thing?" Translation: "You're wrong in what you are saying and I'm innocent. You're being too hard on me."
4. "Me? What about you? Let's look at what you've been saying and doing." The best defense against change is a strong offense.
5. "You ain't seen nothin' yet!" This is a maddening response. You make a request for a change and the other person retaliates by intensifying the behavior you pointed out. Your request is purposely thrown back in your face. The other person may even go out of the way to show you he or she won't change. Your request is rejected in a very obvious manner.

People resist change for many reasons, but there is one basic factor behind them all. When you request that individuals change their behavior, you may be challenging a pattern of behavior they have been following for years. Their established patterns of interacting with other people, responding to situations, and performing tasks are deeply rooted in their self-identity. It's their way of saying, "This is who I am." A request for change becomes a threat to their self-image and they wonder, *What's wrong with me? Haven't I been okay?*

Think about it for a minute. When someone asks you to change, how do you feel about yourself at that moment? Doesn't your sense of self-worth rise defensively within you? For most people, that's exactly what happens. The way change is requested or demanded of us often leaves us feeling that we are wrong or less than we should be. When a request for change threatens or destroys a means by which our self-esteem has been affirmed, our normal response to the change will be resistance.

The key to overcoming resistance to change is in how change is presented. A person is usually open to change when it is presented as an enhancement to his or her self-image instead of a threat to it. This approach promises greater potential for change than any other method. (It is true that, in some destructive behavioral patterns, a crisis event is a more effective approach. But for our purposes, self-image enhancement is recommended. To learn the principles involved in creating a minor or major crisis, see my book, *How to Have a Creative Crisis*, published by Word, Inc.)

Enhancing another's self-image involves encouragement and affirmation. You must believe in the person and view him or her as God does. That's a tall order, but the alternatives are almost nonexistent. Consider what Michael McGill says about the subject in his interesting book, *Changing Him, Changing Her*:

> The reason why people change is that they are made to believe that their new behavior will enhance their self-image, they will be affirmed, rewarded. . . . It is only when others actually *experience* affirmation of their self-image as a result of their new behavior that they will fully integrate this behavior into their behavioral repertoire. And how does that experience come? It comes in the sustained reinforcement and reward that's offered them as a result of their changing. That experience must be a rather overwhelming one to overpower their ingrained experience with their old behavior. They must be convinced that the change really has worked to their betterment and not their detriment. In the absence of such rewarding, reinforcing, reaffirming kind of experience, the chances are they will revert to their prior behavior, much to our consternation and chagrin.[2]

If you've been looking for a simple answer to the question, "How can I effect a change in someone?" there it is. But remember: The emphasis in this book is not on developing creative and clever ways to get *others* to change. If any change occurs in someone you relate to, it will happen because of the change in *you*. We should continually be making changes in our lives to grow, mature, and conform to the teachings of the Word of God in our lives.

I tend to resist change; perhaps you do, too. But did you realize that by pressing through to make personal changes and by allowing the Word of God to fashion your way of relating to others who need to change, your self-image will be enhanced? The Scriptures are with us, not to hinder us or tear us down, but to make our lives better. The more the Word of God comes alive in our lives, the better we will feel about ourselves and the better we will relate to other people. How can you turn down an offer like that!

Difficult but Possible

We agree that it is difficult to get others to change, so we must change ourselves to get along with our unchanging family members and friends. Change is no less difficult for us than it is for them, but it is possible. Let's explore why change, even for us, is so difficult.

Imagine that you're aboard an airplane heading for a destination across the country. After half an hour of flying, you notice the co-pilot strolling down the aisle chatting with the passengers. You think, *That's all right; the pilot is flying the plane.* But then the pilot appears in the aisle alongside the co-pilot. "Who's flying the plane?" you ask the pilot as he walks by. "Don't worry," he responds. "We're on automatic pilot. It flies the plane better than we do. It reacts and responds to flying conditions without having to think."

Many people find change difficult because they live their lives on automatic pilot. They don't really think about what they do or say. They have an entire repertoire of pre-programmed responses tucked within them. Whenever they encounter a situation or a relationship, they react without having to think. Whatever is programmed into them just happens. We are all creatures of habit to a great extent. We may like to think we're flexible, but so many things we do take little or no thought. We develop habits over the years. We may not be aware of how deeply ingrained those patterns are until we catch ourselves doing them almost unconsciously.

I play racquetball every Tuesday, Wednesday, and Thursday morning before going to work. To drive to the club, I just steer the car east on Interstate 405 to highway 22, then turn north on highway 57. I really don't think about it very much. The car seems to know where it's going. But occasionally I need to go to the Orange County Airport by staying on Interstate 405. I am so used to turning north on 22 that I must consciously tell myself, "Stay on 405. Do not take 22 or you will end up at the office or the racquetball club instead of the airport."

Habits operate outside the conscious mind, whereas our choices come from within the conscious mind. As much as 98 percent of what we do is habit rather than choice. Whatever you do again and again becomes a habit. If you smile at your co-workers every morning, it will become a habit. If you respond with defensiveness each time your employees question you, it will become a habit.

Here's the rule: Whatever you practice, you become. If you argue with people regularly, you become an argumentative person. If you criticize people often, you become a critical person. If you keep bringing work home from the office, you become a workaholic. Repeated behaviors become habits. And are you aware of what it takes to change a habit pattern? To replace a negative behavior with a positive one, you need a minimum of eighteen days of conscious repetition of that behavior to give it a chance to lock into your system. A habit seems to have a life of its own. Just like every living being, a habit will fight to stay alive. When you try to change a pattern of behavior, your habit will resist the change. Changing behavior patterns is a massive battle. It can only be won when you focus on replacing old, negative behaviors with positive, new behaviors.[3]

A Plan for Change

Who runs your life, you or your habits? A counselee once said to me, "Norm, I feel as though there is a battle raging inside me. I want to change the way I respond to my parents when they visit or call, but it's a real struggle. It's as if I have declared war on myself." The apostle Paul described the war between what we want to do and what we should do in Romans 6:12–23. Whenever you embark on a campaign to replace an old pattern with a new behavior, plan on a battle.

There will be times of trying to change when you feel overwhelmed by your deeply entrenched habits and want to lift the white flag of surrender. But rejoice: You can change! You can change your way of responding to other people and your success in changing has nothing to do with the way they behave. But to do so, you must avoid the common, self-defeating statement, "Boy, it's hard to change!" Every time you make that statement you reinforce in your mind the difficulty of what you are trying to do. Yes, change is difficult, but it is possible. If you must say, "It's hard to change," always add, "but it can be done."

You cannot expect different results in your relationships from the same old ways of responding to others. New results come from new behaviors or responses. And the new results will primarily be in you, not in others. Here's the key thought I want you to reflect on every day for the next month: Your relationships will change when you change your ways of interacting with and responding to others. When other people change in response to the changes in you, it's merely icing on the cake.

Now let's apply these principles to a present relationship you would like to improve. The following questions will help you review what you have wanted to see happen and what you have already tried. Then you will determine how you can respond in this relationship in the future.

1. Who is the person with whom you are trying to get along better?

2. In what ways would you like this relationship to improve? Please be specific. (Please notice that I did not ask what bothers you about this person, but how you would like the relationship to be different. Focusing on the outcome rather than the problem makes a difference.)

3. How does the other person feel about the relationship? What are his or her expectations? How do you know what his or her expectations are?

4. What have you tried in the past to improve this relationship? What were the results?

5. What are you doing now that is keeping the relationship from improving? What are you doing that is reinforcing the behavior you want to see changed in the other person?

6. What personal habit patterns of response to this person would you like to change?

7. What is the other person doing that makes it difficult for you to respond differently?

8. How will you make your changes apart from the other person's responses?

9. How will you respond if the other person never changes?

10. What passages from the Word of God would you like to apply to your life to assist in improving this relationship?

11. How do you see yourself living out these verses in your relationship with the other person? Describe your plan in detail.

12. How will you pray for the other person? What thoughts will you keep in your mind about him or her?

4

Getting Personal about Loving People

One day, three different counselees came into my office separately with the same problem to share. It was uncanny how closely their stories paralleled each other. In fact, each counselee opened his session by saying, "Norm, I don't feel loved." One person was just beginning a dating relationship, the second had been engaged for over a year, and the third had been married for twenty-three years. Each counselee related a similar struggle: "The special person in my life says he loves me. If it's true, why don't I feel loved? Yes, he performs what he thinks are loving deeds, but they just don't register with me. It's as if he doesn't know how to love me in the ways I need to be loved. I wish he would ask what love means to me or how I want to be loved. If he just knew how to love me we would get along much better."

Perhaps you've felt this way. Certainly others around you have. Parents say "I love you" to their children. Children say "I love you" to their parents. Friends, lovers, and spouses say "I love you" to each other. But when you don't know what love means to the other person, the words may seem empty to him or her. In our endeavors to get along with people, it is important that we take time to discover what others perceive as love.

Love is the key ingredient in any deep personal relationship such as marriage, family, or friendship. Love involves decision, commitment, and feelings. And the goal for love in a relationship is to make it work in practical ways so that individuals get along with each other better. But if you define love differently than does the other person in the relationship, and you express love in your terms instead of his or hers, the relationship may deteriorate instead of improve. You need to know what your partner considers important in the relationship. You need to understand how he or she wants to be cared for, ministered to, nurtured, and loved. One writer states, "Without this knowledge, working on our relationship is like being in a boxing ring with the world champion—and being blindfolded."[1]

Each individual in a relationship needs to answer three important questions for the others involved if love is to reach its goal of helping people get along:

> 1. What does it mean to you to be loved? What does it mean to your partner to be loved?
> 2. What will it take for you to feel loved? What will it take for your partner to feel loved?
> 3. What are you asking of your partner in this regard? What is your partner asking of you in this regard?

In a nonromantic partnership such as a friendship or a work relationship, you can ask the same questions by substituting the words "cared for" or "appreciated" for "loved."

What It Means to Be Loved

Several characteristics of love are common to all successful relationships. These characteristics comprise the responses people have given to the three questions above. As you think about getting along with almost anyone, reflect on these characteristics and look for ways to put them into practice.

Safety and Security. People want to feel safe and secure in their relationships. They want to be able to breathe a sigh of relief among others and say, "It's nice to relax with someone, let down the protective armor, and be myself." This is the characteristic we enjoy so much in friendships and search for so desperately in the business environment. Often the atmosphere surrounding work relationships is heavy with competition. Profits and advancement take priority over interpersonal care and concern. You will get along better with your co-workers when they know that you are not trying to use them as stepping stones to the top.

In which of your relationships do you feel most safe and secure? Who are the people who best convey this characteristic? What do they do that communicates safety and security to you?

Support. People want and need to feel supported by those who care for them. It helps to know you're not facing the world alone. You can depend on others to stand with you in difficult times, even when they don't necessarily agree with your stand. Do you have some supportive persons in your life? Are you a supportive person to them?

A supportive person is not only needed during difficult times, but also during good times. When you support others, you encourage and help them to dream and grow, even to the point they exceed your own level of growth or ability. You use your strengths, capabilities, and skills to lift them above themselves. For example, occasionally I meet some of my former students from Talbot Seminary and discover that they have excelled in some areas of their lives beyond my own level of ability or achievement. That's wonderful! Also, being an avid fisherman, I receive tremendous satisfaction helping others enjoy fishing by learning the skills (yes, there's more to fishing than luck!) which will help them haul in the big ones. And if they catch more fish than I do as a result of the support I give them, all the better!

Loy McGinnis shares an interesting story about a seventy-four-year-old man he met at an executive club in Toronto. The man had just retired from a lifelong career of manufacturing lead pencils. Loy thought that making lead pencils for several decades sounded like a boring way to make a living. He said, "I bet you're glad to be getting out of that business."

The man's answer surprised him. "Oh, no. I'm going to miss it very much. And what I'm going to miss the most are the friends I've made over the past 40 years. My suppliers and customers have been my best friends. And several of the upper level managers of the company are men I hired right out of college. I've enjoyed a great amount of satisfaction from helping them succeed."[2]

That's the key to support: discovering the strengths of others and building on those qualities to help them succeed. To do this, you need a positive attitude toward others. You must look for the best in people. You must believe in people until they believe in themselves and start succeeding. It happens all the time in my counseling office. I see shattered families and individuals who are broken, troubled, and hurting. Often I need to loan them my hope and faith until they can generate some of their own. I must support them by believing in them, their strengths, and their future until they are stable enough to believe for themselves.

Sense of belonging. We all have a built-in, God-given need to belong, and we all know the pain of being excluded or rejected. The sense of belonging comes from being included by others. It makes you feel significant because someone else has opened his or her own private world to you. It's easy to get along with those who accept you, open their hearts to you, and include you in their lives.

The older I get, the more value I place on the sense of belonging I enjoy with my wife and a few close friends. I can share my hurts, my dreams, my thoughts, and my feelings with these people without fear of being put down, laughed at, or rejected. It feels so comfortable to belong. Having received the benefits of belonging, I want to help others to feel included. I realize as a professional counselor, I am paid to do that for some people. But the most important area for including others is among the people I meet outside my office.

Care. Everyone needs somebody to care about and nurture him or her. When you nurture someone, you invite him or her to take a special place in your heart. You express your care through your words as well as your deeds. When you really care about someone, you are willing to move out of your comfort zone for that person's benefit. It's almost impossible not to get along with someone who genuinely cares for you.

I recently discovered an interesting illustration of caring for one another in a Chinese fable:

A very old man knew that he was going to die very soon. Before he died, he wanted to know what heaven and hell were like, so he visited the wise man in his village.

"Can you please tell me what heaven and hell are like?" he asked the wise man.

"Come with me and I will show you," the wise man replied.

The two men walked down a long path until they came to a large house. The wise man took the old man inside, and there they found a large dining room with an enormous table covered with every kind of food imaginable. Around the table were many people, all thin and hungry, who were holding twelve-foot chopsticks. Every time they tried to feed themselves, the food fell off the chopsticks.

The old man said to the wise man, "Surely this must be hell. Will you now show me heaven?"

The wise man said, "Yes, come with me."

The two men left the house and walked farther down the path until they reached another large house. Again they found a large dining room and in it a table filled with all kinds of food. The people here were happy and appeared well fed, but they also held twelve-foot chopsticks.

"How can this be?" said the old man. "These people have twelve-foot chopsticks and yet they are happy and well fed."

The wise man replied, "In heaven the people feed each other."[3]

Acceptance. I want to be accepted by others and so do you. When we accept others for who they are, we free them from the pressure of being molded into the persons we want them to be. When you accept others, you become compatible with them and get along with them, whether as marriage partners, college roommates, or co-workers.

When I counsel couples who are planning to marry, one of the main themes I address is the need to discover, understand, and accept individual differences. But some individuals come with hidden agendas. A woman may say she accepts her fiancé's differences, but her hidden goal is to change him into her ideal image of a man after they are married. She says she accepts him when she is merely tolerating him. There's a big difference. Tolerance says, "I accept you for now, but if you don't change in time, my offer of acceptance will expire." But acceptance says, "I accept you for who you are"—period. No strings attached. When others know you totally accept them, they will be easy to get along with.

Specialness. Have you ever been made to feel that you were a special person? Has anyone treated you as someone completely set apart and prized? Do you have someone in your life who makes you feel like you are precious and valuable? Did you get along with that person? Of course you did! When we communicate to others their specialness to us, there will be little that can block the growth of a positive, caring relationship.[4]

Loving the Unlovely

It's easy for us to love and get along with the attractive, intelligent, neat, and articulate persons around us. But many of the people God calls us to love do not fit into those acceptable classifications. Tony Campolo tells a story which beautifully illustrates what can happen when we reach out to love the unlovely:

> Teddy Stallard certainly qualified as "one of the least." Disinterested in school. Musty, wrinkled clothes; hair never combed. One of those kids in school with a deadpan face, expressionless—sort of a glassy, unfocused stare. When Miss Thompson spoke to Teddy he always answered in monosyllables. Unattractive, unmotivated, and distant, he was just plain hard to like. Even though his teacher said she loved all in her class the same, down inside she wasn't being completely truthful.
>
> Whenever she marked Teddy's papers, she got a certain perverse pleasure out of putting X's next to the wrong answers and when she put the F's at the top of the papers, she always did it with a flair. She should have known better; she had Teddy's records and she knew more about him than she wanted to admit. The records read:

1st Grade: Teddy shows promise with his work and atti-tude, but poor home situation.
2nd Grade: Teddy could do better. Mother is seriously ill. He receives little help at home.
3rd Grade: Teddy is a good boy but too serious. He is a slow learner. His mother died this year.
4th Grade: Teddy is very slow, but well-behaved. His father shows no interest.

Christmas came and the boys and girls in Miss Thompson's class brought her Christmas presents. They piled their presents on her desk and crowded around to watch her open them. Among the presents there was one from Teddy Stallard. She was surprised that he had brought her a gift, but he had. Teddy's gift was wrapped in brown paper and was held together with Scotch tape. On the paper were written simple words, "For Miss Thompson from Teddy." When she opened Teddy's present, out fell a gaudy rhinestone bracelet, with half the stones missing, and a bottle of cheap perfume.

The other boys and girls began to giggle and smirk over Teddy's gifts, but Miss Thompson at least had enough sense to silence them by immediately putting on the bracelet and putting some of the perfume on her wrist. Holding her wrist up for the other children to smell, she said, "Doesn't it smell lovely?" And the children, taking their cue from the teacher, readily agreed with "oo's" and "ah's."

At the end of the day, when school was over and the other children had left, Teddy lingered behind. He slowly came over to her desk and said softly, "Miss Thompson . . . Miss Thompson, you smell just like my mother . . . and her bracelet looks real pretty on you, too. I'm glad you liked my presents." When Teddy left, Miss Thompson got down on her knees and asked God to forgive her.

The next day when the children came to school, they were welcomed by a new teacher. Miss Thompson had become a different person. She was no longer just a teacher; she had become an agent of God. She was now a person committed to loving her children and doing things for them that would live on after her. She helped all the children, but especially the slow ones, and especially Teddy Stallard. By the end of the school year, Teddy showed dramatic improvement. He had caught up with most of the students and was even ahead of some.

She didn't hear from Teddy for a long time. Then one day, she received a note that read:

Dear Miss Thompson:
*   I wanted you to be the first to know. I will be graduating second in my class.*
*   Love,*
*   Teddy Stallard*

Four years later, another note came:

Dear Miss Thompson:
*   They just told me I will be graduating first in my class. I wanted you to be the first to know. The university has not been easy, but I liked it.*
*   Love,*
*   Teddy Stallard*

And four years later:

Dear Miss Thompson:
*   As of today, I am Theodore Stallard, M.D. How about that? I wanted you to be the first to know. I am getting married next month, the 27th to be exact. I want you to come and sit where my mother would sit if she were alive. You are the only family I have now; Dad died last year.*
*   Love,*
*   Teddy Stallard*

Miss Thompson went to that wedding and sat where Teddy's mother would have sat. She deserved to sit there; she had done something for Teddy that he could never forget.[5]

The Teddy Stallards in your life need love too. They need to feel your support, acceptance, and caring. They need to feel special. Who knows what great things your love will release in their lives?

Counterfeit Caring

As you learn to get along with others by reaching out to them in love, keep your motives in clear focus. There are some people who constantly give of themselves to help others, but their efforts are not motivated by love for others. They are caring, helping people because such activity meets their own set of inner needs. They need to help others in order to feel good about themselves. They are hooked on helping. They are "helpoholics." Though he or she may appear to be developing loving relationships with others, the helpoholic is a counterfeit, caring for others only as long as it meets his or her own needs.

Helpoholics come in two varieties: pleasers and rescuers. Each one gives the appearance of genuine love and caring, but neither meets the true test for a caring relationship.

Pleasers. Pleasers live to make other people happy. They appear to be very conscientious and caring. They go out of their way to make others feel comfortable. They're especially good at remembering to do the little things others overlook. The pleasers' response to others seems to reflect all the admirable qualities of caring we want to express.

But pleasers go far beyond what they need to do. For them, caring is not a voluntary act; it's a responsibility. They feel personally responsible for the happiness of others. When people around them are unhappy, the pleasers feel guilty. They think they've failed! This fear of failure drives them to comply with unrealistic requests for their help. It doesn't matter if they have time or not, they do it. They tend to overschedule their calendars and overextend their endurance. They can't say no to anyone because to do so would mean personal failure. I've seen many ministers experience burnout under the pleaser mentality. They run themselves ragged trying to please a congregation that expects its caring pastor to be available at all hours.

Some pleasers overinvest themselves in one person or project. For example, we often applaud parents who pour their time and energy into meeting their children's every "need." But it's not the children's needs which drive these parents; it's their own. They must please their children, their spouses, and their communities as model parents in order to retain their self-esteem. Sometimes the pleasers' inner needs are hidden to them. Their lives are swamped with the urge to care for someone—or for everyone!—but they don't know why and they don't know how to escape.

Carmen Renee Berry has identified two types of pleasers. One is the *organizing pleaser*. These pleasers are adept at organizing themselves, other people, events, and situations in order to please those around them. Organizing pleasers travel through life at a fast pace, but meet their many responsibilities through careful organization.

The second variety, the *spontaneous pleaser*, doesn't make plans months in advance as the organizing pleaser does. He or she simply reaches out and helps whenever help is needed. They are driven to meet the needs of everyone they meet during the day. Often spontaneous pleasers over-commit themselves and suffer great agony when they cannot meet all the needs around them.

Pleasing behavior is an addiction. Strong words? Yes, but they are true. Pleasers are trying to accomplish the impossible by meeting the needs of everyone to validate their own worth. Carmen Berry says, "Pleasers dance to someone else's tune with feet entangled in frustration and in denial of true feelings."[6]

Pleasers don't get along well with others because many of their acts of caring are counterfeit. Pleasers say and do what they think others want them to say and do. They don't really share who they are or what they think or feel. Genuine relationships are sacrificed on the altar of gaining the approval of others by pleasing them. Make sure your acts of caring spring from a sincere love for others, not a compulsive sense of responsibility that says, "I must make others happy."

Rescuers. When I was in high school and college, some of my friends had summer jobs as lifeguards on the beaches or at public pools. To me, lifeguarding was a dream job. These guys were in the sun all day, usually surrounded by crowds of students their own age. The hours were good and the scenery was great!

As summer came to an end, I would say to them, "What a terrific summer job you had! I'll bet you're sorry it's over."

Many of them surprised me with their responses. "Not really. I'm glad to be getting back to school because I am tired of rescuing people."

You can probably identify with the relief my friends felt at no longer being responsible to watch for and rescue floundering swimmers all day. But are you aware that there are people who never tire of rescuing others? In fact, they live for it. They are the rescuers, a second variety of compulsive helpers, who are drawn to people in trauma or crisis. Rescuers seem to be addicted to personal disasters. They seem to wander through life looking for people who need a lifeline or a safety net. They are often attracted to organizations which are dedicated to help hurting people. But, like pleasers, rescuers help others to help themselves. Their caring is merely an effort to meet their own ego needs.

Rescuers are counterfeit carers. They tend to become overinvolved with people who are hurting and they may not follow through with some of their responsibilities. Thus they may seem to be unreliable friends. They make many personal sacrifices to rescue others. They may dread hearing the phone ring at 2:00 A.M., but they must answer it and do whatever is necessary to help someone in need. They may feel trapped in their lifestyle of flitting from tragedy to tragedy to help people, but they are driven to do so and often cannot understand why.

It's true that, on the surface, rescuers are doing what we should all do: helping others through difficult times. But rescuers tend to exceed the proper boundaries for care-giving and end up immersed in the lives of those in crisis. Genuine care-givers minister to those in need out of the abundance of love they wish to give. Rescuers serve others for what they will receive, such as the accolades of people looking on. Also, rescuers may be tempted to prolong others' problems to foster their dependence, further meeting the rescuers' own needs for attention or recognition.[7]

Are You a Genuine Helper?

How can you tell if your attempts at love and caring are genuine or the expression of a helpoholic compulsion? To help you answer this question, I suggest you evaluate your caring thoughts, feelings, and actions using the following statements. For each statement, rate yourself from 1 to 10. A "1" signifies that the statement definitely *does not* reflect you, "10" means it definitely *does* reflect you, "5" is somewhere in the middle, etc. For any statements you rate above "5," please indicate why you tend to reflect this characteristic.

_____ I think and feel responsible for other people—their feelings, thoughts, actions, choices, wants, needs, well-being, lack of well-being, and ultimate destiny.

_____ I feel anxiety, pity, and guilt when other people have a problem.

_____ I feel compelled—almost forced—to help that person solve his problem by offering unwanted advice, giving a series of suggestions, or trying to fix his feelings.

_____ I feel angry when my help isn't effective.

_____ I anticipate other people's needs.

_____ I wonder why others don't anticipate needs.

_____ I find myself saying yes when I mean no, doing things I don't really want to do, doing more than my share of the work, and doing things other people are capable of doing for themselves.

_____ I often don't know what I want or need. When I do know, I tell myself that what I want or need is unimportant.

_____ I try to please others instead of myself.

_____ I find it easier to feel and express anger for injustices done to others than for injustices done to me.

_____ I feel safest when I'm giving.

_____ I feel insecure and guilty when somebody gives something to me.

_____ I feel sad because I spend my whole life giving to others and nobody gives to me.

_____ I find myself attracted to needy people.

_____ I find needy people attracted to me.

_____ I feel bored, empty, and worthless when I don't have a crisis in my life, a problem to solve, or someone to help.

_____ I abandon my routine in order to respond to someone in trouble or do something for someone else.

_____ I overcommit myself.

_____ I feel harried and pressured.

_____ I believe deep inside that other people are responsible for me.

_____ I blame others for the spot I am in.

_____ I believe that other people make me feel the way I do.

_____ I believe other people are making me crazy.

_____ I feel angry, victimized, unappreciated, and used.

_____ I find other people become impatient or angry with me for all the preceding characteristics.

If you tended to respond to these statements with a "6" or above, you may be what is called a codependent. Your life reflects the negative traits of the pleasers and the rescuers. As such, you will find it difficult to develop relationships which will be fulfilling for you. Your chances of getting along with people are minimal until these issues are confronted and worked through. I would like to suggest several resources which may help you in your journey to becoming a genuine caregiver. I recommend *When Helping You Is Hurting Me* (Harper and Row), by Carmen Renee Berry, especially the chapter, "How to Escape the Messiah Trap." Another helpful book is *Codependent No More* (Harper and Row), by Melody Beattie.

When you express genuine love, you will get along better with people. Love can be expressed in many practical ways. Joe Bayly wrote about the action of love in a way that makes sense. His prayer is called, "A Psalm of Single-mindedness." It is simple and to the point, and it has a message for us:

Lord of Reality
make me real
not plastic
synthetic
pretend phony
an actor playing out his part
hypocrite.
I don't want
to keep a prayer list
but to pray
nor agonize to find Your Will
but to obey
what I already know
to argue
theories of inspiration
but to submit to Your Word.
I don't want
to explain the difference
between eros and philos
and agape
but to love.
I don't want
to sing as if I mean it
I want to mean it.
I don't want
to tell it like it is
but to be it
like you want it.
I don't want
to think another needs me
but I need him
else I'm not complete.
I don't want
to tell others how to do it
but to do it
to have to be always right
but to admit it when I'm wrong.
I don't want to be a census taker
but an obstetrician
nor an involved person, a professional
but a friend.
I don't want to be insensitive
but to hurt where other people hurt

nor to say I know how you feel
but to say God knows
and I'll try
if you'll be patient with me
and meanwhile I'll be quiet.
I don't want to scorn the clichés of others
but to mean everything I say
including this.[8]

5

It's Just Common Sense . . . or Is It?

"Don't you have any common sense?"

Do you remember hearing that question from some of your elders and peers? I sure do. I've asked it aloud to some people myself—and asked it in my head to several others! Common sense implies that if you just "use your head" in a situation, somehow you'll know what to do. In some situations, common sense is enough. In many other situations, however, something more is needed.

Getting along with other people takes more than common sense. It takes wisdom. By wisdom I mean the ability to discern, to understand, to have insight, and to use good judgment. That's a big order! Some people equate this kind of wisdom with age. But you don't need to wait until you're eighty to be wise. Wisdom doesn't just happen with age. We've all met people who are "wise beyond their years." Wisdom is something which can be worked on and developed. A person who is developing in wisdom will be able to get along with almost anyone.

Wise Up in the Word

Wisdom is the practical translation and application of the Word of God to everyday life. Here are several thoughts

69

about wisdom which I have paraphrased from a great book of wisdom, the Proverbs of the Old Testament:

Get wisdom! Make it your goal (4:5).
 If you make wisdom your goal, you will eventually receive honor (4:8).
 Wisdom which comes from God is worth more than all the wealth you may try to acquire. Nothing can compare with it! (8:11–12).
 Sensible men and women make wisdom their goal. Those who bypass it for what the world has to offer are fools (17:24).
 One of the ways you can show others that you really care for yourself is by developing wisdom (19:8).
 The strength of wisdom is much better than any type of physical strength (24:5).

But what does wisdom have to do with getting along with people? Everything! You need understanding, insight, discernment, patience, and a host of other qualities to read and relate to others. God's wisdom, resident in His Word and available to you through His Spirit, will equip you to get along with people. In this chapter we will consider several specific applications of God's wisdom to our interpersonal relationships.

Special Privileges, Special Responsibilities

You are sitting in an auditorium with several hundred people who, like you, are involved with the same organization. Awards are being announced, and suddenly the president speaks your name as the recipient of the most prestigious award of all. Along with the award come many special benefits. The applause swells and every head turns your way as you rise from your seat and march proudly to the platform. You are singled out from the crowd for a great honor. You are special. Wow!

As wonderful as an experience like this might be, it can't compare to the notoriety and benefits which come from being a Christian. That leads us to our first principle for applying wisdom to our relationships: Wisdom involves understanding how special you are because of all God as done for you. When you begin to comprehend how special you are to God, you'll feel free to relate to people selflessly and confidently.

What has God done for you? Let me remind you of a few of your benefits as found in the first three chapters of Ephesians:

You were *chosen in Christ* before the world began (1:4).

You were *predestined to be God's adopted child* (1:5).

You are *redeemed* through His blood and your sins are *forgiven* (1:7).

You have been *guaranteed eternal life*, as evidenced by the presence of the Holy Spirit in your life (1:14).

You have *hope* in Christ, your *glorious inheritance* (1:18).

You have experienced the *incomparable power* which raised Jesus Christ from the dead and seated Him at God's right hand (1:19–20).

You are the recipient of God's *incomparable grace* which has saved you apart from anything you have done or can ever do (2:8–9).

You now have *access to the Father* through His Spirit (2:18).

You can *know the love of Christ* which will enable you to receive God's fullness (3:19–20). Emphasis added.

Now do you understand how special you are? I suggest that you take a few minutes to read the first three chapters of Ephesians before continuing with this chapter. It will give you an even clearer picture of your specialness.

What does being special have to do with getting along with others? A great deal. Along with the special privileges and benefits we enjoy from being in Christ comes an awesome responsibility. Paul continued his letter to the Ephesians by urging them to "live a life worthy of the calling you have received" (4:1,NIV). Dr. Gene Getz says, "'To live a life worthy' means to walk along a certain path, to follow a prescribed way designed and planned by the Lord for His children."[1] Part of our path of responsibility is to get along with people, especially fellow Christians. Paul instructed the

Ephesians: "Make every effort to keep the unity of the Spirit through the bond of peace" (Ephesians 4:3, NIV). And to the Corinthians he wrote: "I appeal to you, brothers, in the name of our Lord Jesus Christ, that all of you agree with one another so that there may be no divisions among you and that you may be perfectly united in mind and thought" (1 Corinthians 1:10, NIV); "Be of the same (agreeable) mind one with another; live in peace" (2 Corinthians 13:11, AMP).

Some people are turned off by Christianity because believers are not applying the wisdom of these Scriptures to their relationships. Many Christians don't get along with one another. Believers who argue and bicker are doing nothing to draw the watching world to the loving Father. We are exercising wisdom when we choose to follow the teachings of Scripture which govern our relationships regardless of how we feel, regardless of the behavior of other people, and regardless of circumstances. Obedience to Christ is a fitting response to the specialness we enjoy through Him.

Planning to Reach the Goal

If exercising wisdom in getting along with people is our goal, we need a plan to help us reach the goal. We find our plan in the same place we discovered our goal: God's Word. The Bible—especially the New Testament—is full of practical wisdom for helping us get along with people.

Imagine that a Christian friend wrote a letter to you asking your advice for getting along with people. Which New Testament principles would you include in your letter? If fifty people wrote letters of response, each letter would probably contain a different set of valid principles. Here's an example of what such a letter might look like. Notice specific scriptural steps for reaching the goal:

Dear Jim,
Recently you wrote asking for some advice concerning getting along with your family, friends, and co-workers. Here are some guidelines which will apply to all areas.
First, be sure that Jesus Christ is at the center of your life. When your roots go deeply into His love, you will find that your words and actions around others will reflect His love.

Don't play favorites. You may be tempted to spend more time with the attractive, "with it" people. But everyone needs your love and everyone is the same in God's eyes.

Next, watch your mouth. More people get into difficulty by what they say than anything else. Make sure your speech builds people up instead of rips them apart. If your speech reflects God's grace, people will be drawn to you. Watch what you think about people, too, because your thoughts will be reflected in what you say.

Don't draw attention to yourself. Treat others with the soft hands of gentleness. Don't let others get under your skin or provoke you. Realize that everyone thinks differently and acts differently, but you can accept them if Christ's love is within you.

Other people will disappoint you and hurt you. But don't keep score of their wrongs or try to get back at them. Instead, give your feelings to the Lord and treat them with kindness. People respond positively to someone who can overlook hurt or rejection.

Sometimes we have to put up with obnoxious people. They are really starving for genuine love, kindness, and concern. Allow Jesus Christ to meet their needs through you.
Yours truly,
Norm

Here's an exercise which will help you put your getting-along-with-people plan into action. Write several of the following verses, on which the letter above is based, on separate index cards: James 2:3; 3:2; Ephesians 3:17–19; 4:2–3, 29, 31, 32; 5:2; Colossians 3:8, 12–15. (Consider using either the Living Bible or the Amplified Bible for this exercise.) Carry the cards with you and read each verse aloud morning and evening every day for a month. After thirty days of focusing on these verses, you will own them! Once they are inside you, you will be able to see them reflected in your relationships with others.

Words from the Wise

Those who have healthy relationships with others and are capable of getting along with most people use their words wisely. They are living examples of the wise words of

Proverbs on the subject of communication: "A man has joy in making an apt answer, and a word spoken at the right moment, how good it is!" (15:23, AMP). "A word fitly spoken and in due season is like apples of gold in a setting of silver" (25:11, AMP). "Pleasant words are as a honeycomb, sweet to the mind and healing to the body" (16:24, AMP). "He who has knowledge spares his words, and a man of understanding has a cool spirit. Even a fool when he holds his peace is considered wise; when he closes his lips he is esteemed a man of understanding" (17:27–28, AMP).

The words you use connect you to other people. But *how* are you connected: by a cord that binds you together or a barrier which keeps you at a distance? One company decided to do something about words which kept people apart. It established a policy forbidding the mailing of any letters on company letterhead which contained the word *I*. Instead, employees had to use words which shifted the focus from the sender to the receiver: *you, yourself, and yours.* Or they used warm, "together" words like *we, our, and ourselves.* Emphasis was placed on using courteous words which often are missing from our vocabulary: *sorry, promise, please, thank you, and excuse me.*

We also need to avoid "holding back" words. These are words which subtly tend to turn people away because they reflect our perspective rather than the hearer's: *I, me, myself, my, maybe, and later.* For years I've suggested to married couples that the word *later* leads to some of the greatest conflicts in marriage unless it is defined. *Later* tends to convey, "I'm not interested." If we use it to avoid or delay interaction or compliance, it shouldn't be in our vocabulary.

However, even when we're careful in choosing our words, it's important to understand the potential for misuse. For example, shifting the emphasis from "I" to "you" might work well in some situations—and backfire in others.

Remember the experience of renewing your license at the Department of Motor Vehicles or enrolling for college classes? You heard instructions like: "You'll have to get in the other line. Didn't you read the instructions?" or "You'll have to come back Monday morning. We're closing now" or "You must fill out the form first." When we use the word *you* as part of an order or a command, we usually end up punching someone's resistance button. Most people don't like to be told to do anything. And with any request, use the magic words *please* and *thank you.* These words draw people together instead of drive them apart.

You will find it easier to get along with people if you keep your words simple and to the point. If other people need a dictionary or an interpreter to understand you, you won't get through to them. Don't try to impress others with a ten-dollar word when a twenty-five-cent one will do.

Perhaps you've heard about the "impressive" memo an insurance adjustor sent to the main office: "The pressure involved in getting depositions from on-site witnesses for both the claimant and the disputing party has made it necessary to revise the date set for arbitration of the findings upwards of three days with no slippage foreseen." What did he say? "The full report will be on your desk Thursday." Sometimes, instead of making a point, our many words beat the point to death.

To me, "a word fitly spoken" (Proverbs 25:11, AMP) indicates that you mean what you say. Have you said, "Let's get together sometime" or "I'll give you a call sometime"? It's better either to be specific in what you say or don't use phrases like these at all. When you use vague statements like these without following through on them, you may gain a reputation for being unreliable.[2]

Asking Wisely

The flight attendant noticed that two of her boarding passengers were from the same company, but that they sat several rows apart, even though the plane was only half full. Curious, she asked one of the men why they weren't sitting together.

"I avoid him as much as possible," he answered curtly. "I've worked with him for years and he never changes. He talks incessantly and pesters me with his manipulative questions. I don't enjoy conversing with him."

Questions are an important part of human interaction. Some people use questions to deepen and enrich their relationships. But many people use questions as a weapon to pry, maneuver, gain advantage, attack, trap, set up, or break down the defenses of others. Also, a person who constantly barrages others with questions may be trying to keep others from getting close to him. Some questions are like barriers which keep people from getting along with each other.

Some offensive questions are accusatory, putting people on the spot: "Why did you say that?" "Why do you act that way?" "Why do you always want the same thing for dinner each night?" "Why do you live in such a bad area of town?" Most of us avoid people whose questions reflect accusation and judgment instead of concern and empathy.

Other questions are intended to trap or "set up" people. Have you heard—or asked—questions like these?: "If I can show you a quicker way to do it, would you be interested?" "You want to be healthy and alert when you get older, don't you?" "Wouldn't you just love for me to take you to that overly expensive resort sometime?" "Why won't you take on that second job? You need the extra money to take care of us, don't you?" Questions like these make people feel like they are being backed into a corner and forced to respond a certain way.

A subtle form of trap questions are called closed questions. Closed questions do not invite an opinion, but rather they seek agreement with the asker's opinion. Notice the subtle difference:

> Closed: "Didn't you just love the minister's sermon this morning?"
> Open: "What did you think of the minister's sermon this morning?"
> Closed: "Can you believe our treasurer wanted to spend so much money on the annual banquet?"
> Open: "How did you respond to our treasurer's suggestion regarding banquet expenses?"
> Closed: "Isn't this restaurant awful?"
> Open: "How do you like the restaurant?"

Direct, open, honest, inviting questions will draw people toward you instead of prompt them to avoid you.[3]

A Person of Understanding

A term often used in the Bible in conjunction with wisdom is *understanding*. Proverbs 18:2 reads: "A (self-confident) fool has no delight in understanding, but only in revealing his personal opinions and himself" (AMP). This person is not concerned about getting along with others or listening to others. He is so intent on drawing attention to himself that he doesn't take time to understand the aspects of a situation, problem, or relationship. In contrast, a person of understanding keeps an outward focus in order to discern his supportive role in situations and relationships. The writer of Proverbs extolled the benefits of understanding: "Happy—blessed, fortunate and enviable—is the man who finds skillful and godly Wisdom, and the man who gets understanding—drawing it forth [from God's Word and life's experiences]. For the gaining of it is better than the gaining of silver, and the profit of it than fine gold" (3:13–14, AMP).

A major characteristic of a person of understanding is revealed in Proverbs 14:29: "He who is slow to anger has great understanding, but he who is hasty of spirit exposes and exalts his folly" (AMP). A person who lacks wisdom and understanding will have difficulty controlling his anger. And a person who cannot control his anger will have difficulty getting along with people. Explosive anger has been called the curse of interpersonal relationships. An expression of anger should always be tempered by the relationships it will affect.

Consider the following four facts about anger:

1. Anger is not the real problem or the main emotion. Anger is a symptom. Anger stems either from hurt, fear, or frustration. For many people, frustration tops the list.

2. Expressing anger to another person does not decrease it. Usually an angry outburst increases the emotion and reinforces the tendency for future outbursts to occur.

3. The way you handle your anger is learned. This also means you can learn new ways of expressing and controlling your anger.

4. The other person is *not* responsible for making you angry. You are responsible! (If you want to know more about

anger and what to do about it, read chapter eleven in my book, *Making Peace with Your Partner*, published by Word.

Proverbs 18:13 reveals a major element of misunderstanding which contributes to our anger: "What a shame—yes, how stupid!—to decide before knowing the facts" (TLB). We often make judgments before considering all the facts. We think we know all we need to know and we react to the situation without understanding, often in anger. However, a person of understanding takes time to observe, investigate, and see the situation empathetically through the eyes of others.

Consider the following situations. How would a hasty, thoughtless person respond? How would a person of understanding respond? How would you respond?

> You arrive on time for your appointment, but you sit in the waiting room for over an hour before the doctor can see you.
> A business acquaintance sets a lunch date with you, then fails to show up at the restaurant.
> Your spouse promises to run an important errand for you, but forgets to do so.
> You loan a tool to your neighbor who promises to return it by Saturday so you can use it. He fails to return it.
> One of your employees leaves work a few minutes early each day for several weeks with no explanation.

What is your first thought in each of these situations? Do you tend to jump to conclusions? For example, you may think the doctor is so interested in making money that he overscheduled, causing you to wait. You may imagine your business friend was preoccupied with someone he or she liked better than you. Your spouse judged your errand to be unimportant and ignored it. Your neighbor hoped you would forget he had the tool so he could keep it. Your employee was trying to cheat you out of some work time.

Perhaps you would respond in one or more of the following ways:

> You become angry at others for being inconsiderate.
> You make statements to yourself such as, "I can't believe that person could be so thoughtless."

You gripe about it to three other people that day.

You vow that you will never get involved in that situation again.

You look for a way to make the other person pay for his or her thoughtlessness.

You consider changing doctors, firing the employee, chewing out your neighbor, etc.

You ask yourself, "I wonder what really happened. There is probably a good explanation for this problem. I need to find out what it is. I will talk with him or her about it. In the meantime, I will pray for that person."

You see, you have a number of different options for responding to irritating situations. Some lead to anger and perhaps to a severed relationship. But the last choice reflects both understanding and the love which "is ever ready to believe the best of every person" (1 Corinthians 13:7, AMP). You can at least see plausible reasons for the situation. Your doctor may have been delayed because of an emergency with another patient. Your business acquaintance may have been ill. Your spouse neglected your errand because he or she was ministering to a non-Christian neighbor. Your neighbor may have needed to use the tool another week and tried unsuccessfully to call you about it. Your employee may have been working through breaks so he or she can leave early for a son's baseball games. Yes, it would have been better had these individuals explained their actions ahead of time. But when that doesn't happen, a person of understanding will always guard the relationship by patiently looking on the bright side.

Persons of understanding will get along with others because they can handle not only their own feelings of anger, but also any anger directed toward them. When others are angry with you, you don't need to withdraw into a cocoon or explode in retaliation. You have several positive alternatives to those reactions.

First, give the other person permission to be angry with you. Tell yourself, "It's okay for him to be angry. I can handle it and I will listen to his concern. What he is sharing right now is not just anger; it's fear, hurt, or frustration. I will try to understand the root of the anger."

Second, don't change your behavior just to keep someone from being angry with you. If you do, you are allowing yourself to be controlled. When someone becomes angry, it is his or her responsibility to deal with it. However, if you are doing something you should not be doing, and someone becomes angry because of it, change your behavior.

Third, don't reinforce the anger of others by responding in kind or by complying with their demands. Simply state your point in a caring, logical manner.

Fourth, ask the person to respond to you in a reasonable manner. Suggest that he or she restate the original concern in a lower tone of voice, and speak to you as if you had just been introduced for the first time. Your request may take the other person by surprise, but it will shift the focus from his or her feelings to the issue at hand.

Fifth, you don't need to respond to anger with anger. Memorize and review often the following passages and you will understand why angry retorts are nonproductive: "A hot-tempered man stirs up strife, but he who is slow to anger appeases contention" (Proverbs 15:18, AMP). "Good sense makes a man restrain his anger, and it is his glory to overlook a transgression or an offense" (Proverbs 19:11, AMP). "Let every man be quick to hear, . . . show to speak, slow to take offense and to get angry" (James 1:19, AMP).

Show a Little Kindness

Do you know what it feels like to be taken for granted? You continue to give of yourself over a period of time and yet there is no response to, or recognition for, your efforts. Even though we should be able to give freely and lovingly without expecting anything in return, most people respond well when their efforts are acknowledged. Being wise and sensitive to recognize and appreciate the contributions of others is a surefire way to get along with them.

Sometimes people need to be gently reminded about the need for sensitivity and appreciation. I remember a wife who knew how to encourage her husband in loving and helpful ways. She said to him, "Honey, if I die before you do, you would spend quite a bit of money on flowers for my funeral, wouldn't you?"

"Of course I would, dear," he answered, somewhat shocked at her question. "Why do you ask?"

"I was just thinking that all the flowers in the world won't mean much to me then. But a little flower from time to time while I'm still alive would sure brighten my days." From that day on she received one beautiful flower each week from her husband. On one hand, it's too bad she had to ask for her husband's recognition through flowers. But on the other hand, being up front with her request was better than letting her wish fester inside.

Over the years, a number of wives have shared with me that the only time they hear anything about the way they care for their husbands is when favorite shirts or clean socks are not in the drawer. And that's usually just one day out of thirty. On the other twenty-nine days, when all the clean clothes are in place, the wives never hear a word of appreciation for their efforts. These women desperately need their husbands to affirm them, compliment them, and thank them in small but meaningful ways.

There are many ways we can pass out "flowers" to brighten the lives of people around us. One practical way is to send notes, cards, and letters expressing love, friendship, appreciation, and thanks to the people in your life. Over the years I have received unsolicited cards and notes from students, seminar participants, and counselees. Each of those kind expressions made my day! It's nice to be appreciated.

For more than three years I have employed two part-time receptionists in my counseling office. Each of them works two days a week. The two women have known Joyce and me, and each other, for more than thirty years, so they complement each other and fit into the office beautifully. They have added so much to our office through their thorough, competent work. But more than that, their sensitivity and attention to the needs and concerns of others is outstanding. They always remember everyone's birthday and special occasions. They are constantly bringing homemade goodies to the office to share with everyone. They express their appreciation through notes, cards, and personal words. They add a healthy dimension of interpersonal comfort to our office. They reflect caring qualities both in what they do and who they are. The careful attention to recognition and appreciation that these women show is important in any type of relationship—home, work, church, neighborhood, friendship, etc.

People are drawn to those who are appreciative and repelled by those who seem indifferent. One survey I read illustrated this point. The survey described the various reasons why customers stopped shopping in a certain department store. One percent of the customers stopped shopping due to death. Three percent moved away from the area and five percent changed stores because of a friend's recommendation. Nine percent left because of competitive prices and 14 percent were not happy with the products. But an overwhelming 68 percent decided to shop elsewhere because of attitudes of indifference expressed by employees. Think about it. When you sense an "I-don't-care" attitude coming from the staff of a restaurant or store, do you feel like patronizing that establishment again? There have been times when I wanted to take waiters or clerks aside for five minutes and talk to them about how their poor attitudes were negatively impacting customers. Negative, indifferent attitudes can ruin all levels of relationships.[4]

I hope by now you have begun to think seriously about the importance of applying scriptural wisdom to your relationships. When you are stumped in your interaction with others, reflect on the Scripture passages presented in this chapter. Ask God for the insight and sensitivity to select specific passages from His Word to implement in those situations. You may not be able to determine what to do on your own, but that's why God shares His wisdom with us, isn't it?

6

Are You Turned on to Tuning In?

In late 1988, worldwide attention was focused on the bleak arctic region near the top of the globe. Three whales were trapped in a tiny circle of ocean surrounded by a huge ice pack. The three creatures were doomed to die unless the ice pack was broken allowing them access to the open sea. Soviet and American icebreakers plowed through the ice in a frantic attempt to free the whales. As the days wore on, one of the whales succumbed and disappeared into the depths. Finally, after spending several days in effort and hundreds of thousands of dollars in resources, rescuers broke through the ice pack and freed the surviving whales. And the watching world breathed a sigh of relief.

Why was so much effort and money spent just to rescue three whales? The answer is summarized in two of the world's most attention-catching words: endangered species! We have become very protective against the potential loss of earth's environmental resources. We have established societies to guard a wide variety of animals and plants which face extinction today. Environmentalists labor tirelessly, and sometimes even militantly, to assure the preservation of endangered species.

Did you realize there is an endangered species in the human family which exists right under our noses? You may have run into one of these people today without realizing how rare they are. We all want to be around these people. We truly enjoy their company; they get along with almost everybody. They make a tremendous impact on those around them. But they are becoming increasingly difficult to find. I'm talking about the endangered species of genuine listeners—people who know how to listen with their eyes, minds, and hearts as well as their ears.

Are you a member of this rare species? Do you qualify as a real listener? You may think you do. But before you answer, are you sure you know what a real listener is? I've counseled people for more than twenty years who thought they were listeners, but were shocked to discover that they didn't fit the description. They hadn't been listening at all! They needed to discover that true listening is a skill which must be learned, practiced, and developed.

People are desperately hungry to be listened to by others. You can probably think of a number of people who talk to you. But who listens to you when you want to talk—I mean *really* listens? And on the other side of the coin, who do you listen to? We would all get along better with others if we knew how to be listeners. But, unfortunately, good listeners are often hard to find.

The dearth of genuine listeners is humorously illustrated by the story of a young psychiatrist who began his practice in a large office building. Every evening, after hearing people talk about their problems all day, the young doctor was exhausted. When he stepped into the elevator to go home, his shoulders were slumped and his head was down. Everything about his posture and expression reflected his utter fatigue.

The elevator always stopped a few floors down and another psychiatrist, who had been practicing for over thirty years, briskly stepped in. The older man always looked perky and alert, wearing a smile on his face and whistling a happy tune. There wasn't a hint of weariness about him. The young psychiatrist was curious about the old doctor's resilience in such a taxing profession, but he said nothing.

The scene was repeated every day for three weeks. The young doctor entered the elevator looking tired and drained, but the veteran psychiatrist was always the picture of vitality. Finally, the young psychiatrist's curiosity got the best of him. "I just don't understand it," he said to his chipper colleague one day as they rode the elevator to the lobby. "I can hardly move after listening to people describe their problems. Yet you leave your office every day just as fresh and energetic as you arrived. All that listening drains me. How do you do it?"

The old psychiatrist smiled and said, "Who listens?"

We may chuckle at the story, but it is so indicative of what happens between people today. People love to talk, but who wants to listen? Often our conversations are simply dialogs of the deaf—everybody talking, but nobody listening! As the elevator story suggests, sometimes professional listeners—pastors, psychiatrists, psychologists, counselors—are among the greatest offenders.

Jesus expressed the problem this way: "This is why I speak to them in parables: 'Though seeing, they do not see; though hearing, they do not hear or understand'" (Matthew 13:13, NIV). We don't really see all that we could be seeing with our eyes, nor do we hear all that we could be hearing with our ears. I notice this lack of listening in our churches. For example, two parishioners greet each other as they arrive on Sunday morning:

"How are you today, Brother Smith?"

"Terrible, Brother Jones. Yesterday my dog was run over by a truck, and both kids have the measles."

"Praise the Lord! That's wonderful, Brother Smith. Have a blessed day."

Am I being facetious? Only slightly. I've seen this kind of thing happen and so have you. It not only happens in churches, it happens everywhere. Take the experience of air travel, for example. When the plane lands and the passengers are filing out, the flight attendants at the door are saying rather mechanically, "Good-bye. Thanks for flying with us. Hope you enjoyed the flight."

Sometimes I jokingly test their listening by responding, "It was a terrible flight. Three of us threw up. Good-bye." Usually they just smile and nod as they turn to greet the next person in line. They're not listening.

A couple of times recently I have given this illustration in seminars I have taught, and flight attendants came up to speak to me afterward. "You're right about flight attendants not listening," they admitted. "It's so boring saying good-bye to hundreds of passengers every day that our brains slip into neutral. What they say to us often doesn't register."

I heard a story about a man who was determined to prove how inattentive people are in their listening. Once, when passing through a receiving line at a wedding reception, he greeted each member of the wedding party with a pleasant expression and a warm smile while saying, "The alligators are loose." Each person he spoke to smiled back and thanked him. One woman even said, "Oh, I'm so glad you like them. I made them myself." People hear, but they don't always listen.

Listening is a fine art. It's a gift of spiritual significance you can learn to give to others. In the Proverbs we read, "The hearing ear and the seeing eye, the Lord has made both of them" (Proverbs 20:12, AMP). When you listen to others you give them a sense of importance, hope, and love that they may not receive any other way. Through listening we nurture and validate the feelings of others, especially when they are experiencing difficulties in life.

Listening is giving sharp attention to what someone else is sharing with you. Notice that I didn't say "what someone else is *saying* to you." Often what others share with us is more than what they say. We must listen to the total person, not just the words he or she speaks. Listening requires openness to whatever others share with us—feelings, attitudes, concerns, etc., as well as words. Listening also means putting yourself in a position to respond to whatever is being shared with you.

Listening is an expression of love since it involves caring enough to take seriously what another person is communicating. When you listen lovingly, you invite that person into your life as a guest. When people know you hear them, they will trust you and feel safe with you. And if you are a good listener, others will be more apt to invite you into their lives as a guest. Those you listen to will also learn through your example to respond openly and lovingly to what you share with them.

Varieties of Listening

Did you know there are at least three kinds of listening? Each variety is a different and necessary expression of the learned skill of listening. Let's look at each of them.

Wordless listening. In wordless listening you use your body posture, the expression on your face and your tone of voice to communicate to another person that you want to hear more about what they are trying to share with you. Listening with a blank, deadpan expression can be annoying or distracting to the speaker. He or she may think you're not paying attention or not interested. You may *say* you're listening, but if you don't *show* you're listening, your "listening" won't be believed. Some kind of physical animation is necessary to communicate your interest nonverbally.

Another element of wordless listening involves your response through sounds of interest. For example, as someone is sharing with you, you can occasionally interject "mmm," "ahh," "yes," "uh-huh," "really," or some other sound which invites the person to continue sharing with you. These responses are not questions or statements, but merely nonjudgmental sounds which communicate, "I hear you; tell me more." Some sounds we offer when listening are not invitations to continue but judgments or challenges of believability. For example, I've heard people respond, "Oh, yeah?" with an inflection in the voice which says, "I don't believe you." Effective wordless listening will always employ postures, expressions, and nonmessage sounds which communicate full attention and cause the speaker to feel comfortable about continuing to share.

During the darkest hours of the Civil War, President Abraham Lincoln wrote to an old friend in Springfield, Illinois, inviting him to come to Washington to discuss some problems. When his friend arrived, Lincoln talked to him about the pros and cons of emancipating the slaves. He read aloud to his friend many letters and newspaper articles on the issue. Some people wrote to denounce the president for not freeing the slaves and others denounced him in fear that he would free them. After several hours the president shook hands with his old friend, said good-bye and sent him back to Illinois. Lincoln had done all the talking. He hadn't even asked his friend's opinion on the issues. "He seemed to feel easier after that talk," the old friend later reported.

Lincoln didn't want advice. He merely wanted a friendly, sympathetic listener with whom he could share his burden. That's usually what is wanted by the troubled people around us—our irritated customers, our dissatisfied employees, our hurting friends. They just need us to listen to them and to communicate nonverbally that we care for them and that we're interested in what they have to say.[1]

Checking listening. Often when listening you need to check with the speaker to see if you are hearing and understanding what he or she really means. In checking you reflect back to the speaker what you heard to verify the message. For example, you may say, "What I hear you saying is (repeat or summarize message). Is this what you meant? Did I understand you correctly?" Checking in this manner gives the speaker an opportunity to clarify any misunderstanding that may have occurred in the giving or receiving of the message. But checking statements must be given with tone of voice and body language which shows interest in the message, not a challenge to it.

Checking listening is a helpful method for dealing with problem communicators such as people who complain or criticize excessively, or those who dominate conversations. Often we try to avoid these unpleasant encounters only to get trapped in them anyway. Our tone of voice and body language reveals to them that we don't enjoy listening to them. But the more we resist, the more they persist. They get the nonverbal message that we're not enjoying the conversation, but it doesn't seem to slow them down.

Why not stop resisting and start listening—really listening in a new way? By checking listening you will be able to take charge of a negative conversation and exert a positive influence over the situation. That's right: The listener, not the speaker, holds the most control, power, and influence in a conversation. If a conversation were a car, the speaker would be the engine and the listener, especially a checking listener, would be the steering wheel. The car's engine provides the power, but the steering wheel decides where the car will go.

The listener who checks the complainer, criticizer, or dominator with questions and statements can direct the conversation.

John came to my office to discuss his difficulty at work. He had all three kinds of problem communicators in his office. These people really needed to talk to John in the course of daily business. But they irritated John so much that he found creative ways to avoid them most of the time, which often provoked more hostility in staff relationships. John loved his job, but he had such a difficult time relating to his abrasive co-workers that he found himself wanting to stay away from the office.

I asked John to give me an example of irritating communication from his fellow workers. He said, "Fred is a complainer. He often whines that he has more territory than he can handle and that he needs help in covering his accounts. I can't stand to hear the same old complaint all the time, so I avoid him as much as possible."

I responded, "Maybe you need to stop avoiding Fred and really listen to him. If he realized that you were listening to him, perhaps he wouldn't bug you so often and your working relationship would improve." Then I shared with him about checking listening and suggested the following sample statements he could use to reflect Fred's complaint back to him: "Fred, you're saying that you have too much to handle by yourself and you need another person to help you." "I understand that your territory is getting too large for one person to handle." "It sounds as if you're overwhelmed right now because your territory is too large."

I encouraged John to come up with his own checking statements and practice them at home until he felt at ease with the process. He felt a little uncomfortable with the new approach at first, but after two months he remarked, "It's working. I can't believe how much the three irritants in my office have changed. When I use checking listening, they don't go on and on like they used to. We've even started talking about personal issues now instead of only work-related issues."

I said to John, "If I asked your three co-workers how *you* have changed, how do you think they would answer?"

John nodded knowingly. "They would say I've become a real listener."

According to Proverbs, there are some sad penalties for not being a good checking listener: "He who answers a matter before he hears the facts, it is folly and shame to him" (Proverbs 18:13, AMP). But on the positive side of the ledger, there are at least six great benefits to checking listening:

1. The speaker will appreciate being heard and understood by you.
2. Checking listening can reduce anger and calm a heated discussion because the speaker realizes he or she is being heard.
3. Miscommunications are minimized or eliminated. Checking listening gives the speaker the opportunity to clarify his or her meaning.
4. The listener who checks with questions or statements will remember what the speaker says much better than with passive listening.
5. Checking listening is one of the most direct and effective ways to eliminate communication problems.
6. Checking listening helps the listener remain calm and feel more in control of the interaction by reducing emotional tension and putting him or her in the driver's seat.

Nurturing listening. In this third variety of listening, you listen for the emotional content behind the message being shared and reflect it back to the speaker in an empathetic manner in your own words. Nurturing listening conveys support, caring, and acceptance for the speaker and his or her point of view. Nurturing listening extends a warm invitation to the speaker to share deepest joys, concerns, or hurts with you.

The following dialog, one of the weekly telephone conversations between Frank and his father, illustrates nurturing listening. Frank's father and mother had been married for fifty-one years before she died nearly three years ago. Frank's father was deeply shaken by his loss and he still doesn't go out much. Many of his friends have encouraged him to continue his hobbies and to stay busy visiting his many grandchildren. Notice how Frank nurtures his father by simply listening and sharing empathetic responses:

Frank: Hi, Dad. How are you doing today?
Dad: I'm getting along just fine, Son.
Frank: You're doing okay then.
Dad: Yes, as well as I can with your mother gone.
Frank: Dad, it sounds like you still feel Mom's passing deeply. It was a real loss.
Dad: You know, I didn't think it was going to be this bad. I didn't think it would take this long to recover.
Frank: After all the years you were together, you miss her and miss the times you had together.
Dad (after a pause, with a slight break in his voice): Frank, I miss her each day, and sometimes I feel lonely all day long. Lots of friends want me to move on with life and not think about her so much. But I want to remember. There are so many good memories.
Frank: You sound like you want to do something to help you remember Mom.
Dad: This may sound dumb, but I really want to visit some of the places Mom and I used to go together. I was thinking about taking one or two of the grandkids with me. What do you think?

Did Frank give his opinion of what his father ought to do? Did he advise his father on a decision? Did he try to cheer up his father? No. He simply listened reflectively in a way which nurtured his father and encouraged him to express his inner thoughts and feelings. Frank's responses made his dad feel understood. That's what people want: someone who understands and accepts them. As you learn to nurture others with your listening, you can fill the need for understanding and acceptance in others.

Notice how nurturing listening can also be used in relating to people at work. Denise is talking with Mary, an older woman who works with her:

Mary: It seems to be getting dark earlier each day.
Denise: Yes, it does seem that way.
Mary: I wish it wasn't getting dark so soon. I have four blocks to walk after I get off the bus and you never know who you'll run into on the streets these days.
Denise: You're afraid something might happen to you.
Mary: I guess I am. I hate to sound like a fearful old woman,

but just last week a younger woman was robbed only a block from my home.

Denise: You're afraid that the same thing could happen to you when you're walking home in the dark.

Mary: Yes, and that's why I want to ask our supervisor to juggle my hours for the next two months so I can get home before dark. I would feel a lot safer.

Denise's nurturing response helped Mary take steps to sharing her real feelings.[2]

The Caring Listener

Since the Word of God calls each believer to be "a ready listener" (James 1:19, AMP), we must understand what it means to listen. There is a difference between listening and hearing. Hearing is basically to gain content or information for your own purposes. In hearing you are concerned about what is going on inside *you* during the conversation. You're tuned in to your own reactions, responses, thoughts, and feelings.

Listening means caring for and empathizing with the person you are listening to. In listening you are trying to understand the thoughts and feelings of the speaker. You are listening for his or her sake, not yours. You are not thinking about what you are going to say when the speaker stops talking. You are not engrossed in formulating your own response. You are concentrating on what is being said.

The caring listener will be sensitive to listen for nonverbal cues from the speaker such as tone, volume, and pitch. These cues will tell when the speaker is open for a response and when he does not want to be interrupted. For example, when voice pitch decreases, the speaker is usually willing to allow someone else to speak. But when his volume and speech rate increase, he is indicating that he wants to continue talking. When a person speaks slowly or softly, he may be revealing that he is sad or reluctant to talk about a sensitive topic. But increasing volume and speech rate may reflect either anger or happiness. Picking up these cues will help the listener know when to speak and when to remain quiet.

Numerous studies suggest that men and women listen

differently. Men tend to utter few listening sounds; women are more liberal in sending these wordless cues and more expectant of receiving them. When men do offer a nonverbal response, they generally indicate "I agree with you." But women take a man's feedback responses to mean "I'm listening." And since the man offers fewer responses than the woman expects, she may think he isn't listening to her.

To complicate the problem further, many people attach additional meaning to these nonverbal cues. For example, to some the response "mmm" not only means "I'm listening to you," but also conveys "I enjoy or care about what you are saying." So a woman may inaccurately interpret a man's lack of response as a lack of caring. Or a man may translate his wife's many responses as interest when she is not enjoying the conversation at all.

Women also tend to ask more questions overall, and more personal questions in particular, than men. Some men think, *If she wants to tell me something, she'll speak up without my asking about it.* But women tend to think, *If I don't ask, he'll think I'm not interested.* Men are more prone to interrupt a conversation with their comments, while women often wait to speak until the other person stops talking.

Since a man often uses "mmm" or other nonverbal cues to indicate agreement, he is apt to think that, when his wife responds in the same way, she is in agreement with him. He may later feel betrayed when he discovers that she wasn't agreeing with him at all. Her nonverbal responses simply indicated that she was interested in what he was saying and she wanted to keep the conversation going. On the other hand, a woman may feel ignored by her husband because of his lack of response. This is why you often hear men complain, "Women say one thing and mean another," while women say, "Men don't listen very well."[3]

Obstacles to Good Listening

Listening that springs from caring builds closeness, reflects love, and expresses grace. Yes, listening is an act of grace. Sensitive listening is an open mine shaft to deeper relationships. But all too often the potential for listening lies untapped within us like a generous vein of unmined gold. We have difficulty employing listening skills because one or more obstacles block their expression or development. Each of us may struggle with these obstacles from time to time. But people whose daily lives are regularly characterized by any of them will usually not be quality listeners.

One obstacle to good listening is defensiveness. A defensive person does not really listen when another speaks, but uses this time to formulate rebuttals, excuses, or exceptions to what is being communicated to him or her. The defensive listener is mentally arguing with the speaker instead of receiving with care and grade what is being shared.

Another form of defensive listening is to interrupt the speaker by voicing a premature conclusion. Jim had been in counseling with me for three sessions before I began using a tape recorder in the session. After a half-hour of the recorded session had passed, I stopped the recorder and said, "Jim, I'm going to play back a portion of the tape. I would like you to listen for awhile and then share with me your observations about our conversation."

As I played the tape, Jim's expression changed from interest to embarrassment, shock, and discomfort. Finally he said, "You can turn it off now, Norm. I realize what I've been doing to you. I finished many of your statements for you, and sometimes my hasty comment was not at all what you intended to say. I do that to everyone I talk to."

"Jim, what are you thinking about when other people are speaking?" I asked.

"I'm mentally jumping ahead of them to premature conclusions. I think I know what they're going to say, so I finish their statements for them to hurry the conversation along."

Interrupting a speaker with your conclusion is easy to do when you feel that you have been through the conversation before and know where the speaker is heading. But often our expectations are wrong, and our persistent defensive interruptions produce a negative effect on communication and relationships.

Other obstacles to listening are the biased attitudes we often hold toward certain individuals or groups. A tone of voice or a particular accent may irritate you, so you tend not to listen to people who speak that way. You may be tempted to ignore someone who reminds you of an unpleasant relationship from your past. You may screen out angry or sarcastic comments because persons with those qualities bother you. You may be more biased toward what is shared by a man than by a woman, or vice versa. You may listen more intently to your superiors than to your subordinates. You may be more interested in the comments from a member of your political party than from someone in the opposing party. Pessimists usually tune in to the bad news while optimists listen more closely to the good news.

Good listening can also be blocked by your emotional involvement with the speaker or the message and its impact on your energy level. One day another counselor told me, "Norm, I've cancelled my last two clients today. I've heard so much already that I feel like all the available space in my brain has been used up. I'm mentally and physically exhausted, and I don't think I'll be a very good listener." He made a wise decision.

Another obstacle to good listening is your mind's tendency to wander. We humans have the capacity to think at five times the rate we can speak. So when someone is speaking to you at about a hundred words per minute, and you are processing the information at five hundred words per minute, you may find your mind wandering. You must learn to pace your listening to the speaker or your mind will take off on a journey of its own.

I like to think I'm a fairly good listener, but I know that my listening skills can improve. We tend to hear what we want to hear and filter out what we don't want to hear, and my filter works just like anyone else's. The mind is a great editor, but sometimes it retains the trifles you hear while ignoring significant information. Don't be discouraged if your listening is not what you want it to be. We all have room for improvement.

Listening with Your Eyes

I want to challenge you to try a listening experiment. This evening, tune your television to one of the many half-hour comedy or drama programs, then turn off the sound and listen. Does that sound like a dumb assignment? It really isn't. I challenge you to listen with your eyes. What are the characters communicating with their facial expressions, their body language, their mannerisms, and other nonverbal signals?

In face-to-face communication, words comprise only seven percent of the message and tone of voice adds another 38 percent. But nonverbal signals and body language make up a commanding 55 percent of the message. When it comes to listening, many people are "eye deaf." We often tune in to the spoken message, but ignore the unspoken message of expressions, posture, and actions.

Our son, Matthew, is retarded. He has no verbal vocabulary. So I have learned to listen to Matthew with my eyes, to read his simple nonverbal messages. Because of my experience with Matthew, I have also learned to listen with my eyes to the messages my counselees cannot put into words. I tune in to the unspoken messages of hurt, frustration, delight, or hope I see in a client's face, posture, and walk. As I reveal to my clients what I see, they are encouraged to explain further what they are thinking and feeling.

In order to read the nonverbal messages from those speaking to us, we must learn to look carefully at the speaker. Many conversations today take place while one or more participants hide behind newspapers or magazines, or stare at a television screen. When you do not look at the speaker, you can miss a large portion of the message. Listening with your eyes will help you become a complete listener.

Whenever the spoken message you are hearing conflicts with the nonverbal message you are seeing, you may want to believe your eyes more than your ears. For example, if someone whose face is flushed red, teeth are clenched, and voice is strained says to you, "I'm not angry," you'd better heed the nonverbal cues! It's easy for most people to lie verbally, but it's difficult to lie nonverbally. That's because our nonverbal statements come from the right side of the brain, and it takes an incredible amount of work to alter them. By listening with your eyes you have the opportunity to respond to the speaker's true feelings and concerns instead of getting caught up in his or her words.

Counselors and students of the communication process listen visually all the time. Sometimes in counseling I will change my focus from what the client is saying to what his body language is telling me. I've learned to make statements and ask questions based on the nonverbal messages I see. I've had people say, "Norm, your question was right on target. How did you know what I was thinking about?" I often respond, "Because you've been telling me about it." Usually, after a thoughtful pause, the person realizes I'm referring to the nonverbal messages which have communicated volumes to me.

Do you know what nonverbal messages to look for as you communicate with others? Pay special attention to heads and faces. A person nodding his or her head while you speak usually is communicating agreement or understanding, or inviting you to continue. We scratch our heads when we are puzzled, or touch our noses when in doubt. Frustrated or angry persons often rub their neck. When you want to interrupt, you often will tug on one of your ears.

If a person's head is up and remains still except for an occasional nod, he or she is generally neutral about what is being said. If the head tilts to one side, the listener is expressing interest. If the listener tilts the head forward or leans forward with chin on hand, you are getting your point across. But when a person's head goes down, it may indicate a negative or judgmental attitude. And if you can't get the listener's head up, you have a communication problem!

Eyebrows can be strong senders of nonverbal messages. Raised eyebrows which are curved and high show surprise. Raised eyebrows which are drawn together may be reflecting fear. When eyebrows are lowered and drawn together, and vertical lines appear between them, watch out! You may be facing an angry person. When the inner corners of the eyebrows are drawn up until they lift the upper eyelids, sadness probably exists.

Hands also are strong communicators to the visual listener. We often wring our hands to convey grief or anxiety. Clenched fists can be a sign of anger or tension. Hands on the hips suggest impatience. Hands behind the back can mean that the person does not feel in control of himself or herself at the moment. Hands locked behind the head often indicate a feeling of superiority. Some people stuff their hands in their pockets when attempting to hide the meaning of their words. Crossed arms can indicate defensiveness. Arms extended forward with palms up can reflect sincerity. Isn't it amazing how much your body can say without you uttering a word?

As you focus on becoming a caring and responsive listener among family members, friends, and co-workers, you will not only get along with people, but you will convey the love of Jesus Christ in a very practical and noticeable way. We want to be people who use our eyes to really see and our ears to really hear others as Christ did. We would do well to pray the following prayer:

> We do not really listen to each other, God. . . . Instead of true dialog, we carry on two parallel monologues. I talk. My companion talks. But what we are really concentrating on is how to sound good, how to make our points strongly. . . . Teach us to listen as your Son listened to everyone who spoke with Him. Remind us that, somehow . . . your truth, your love, your goodness are seeking us out in the truth, love, and goodness being communicated. . . . Teach us to be still, Lord, that we may truly hear.[4]

7

The Fitness of Fitting In

"The place where I work is like a melting pot. We have employees of every size, shape, and style of communication. I have fifteen people working under me and sometimes I feel like a zookeeper who must learn the habits and characteristics of fifteen completely different species of animals in order to get along with them all. I can talk to some of my people and we just click. We understand each other and get along well. But with others of my employees, I try to communicate and you'd think I was speaking in a foreign language. We don't click. We'd all get along better if we weren't so different."

Have you ever said something like that about the people you work with, live with, or go to church with? Sure you have, and so have many others wherever different kinds of people try to get along. Is it possible to relate to people who are different from us? Yes! You have two options. First, you can commit yourself to the lifetime project of trying to remake everyone you know to be more like you. Yes, you're right: I'm being facetious. There is no way you can change everybody to be like you. So you really only have one option, and that's to become flexible enough to fit in with the people you can't change.

Some think flexibility is the art of changing colors like a chameleon, losing one's identity in order to blend in with others. That's defensive and manipulative. It's also unhealthy, as it was for the chameleon who died trying to accommodate himself to scotch plaid! Rather, I suggest that we become sensitive to people and situations, and learn to relate flexibly to those who are different from us. Such flexibility is not defensive or manipulative, but a response based on the vital qualities of genuineness, nonpossessive love, and empathy explained in chapter one.

Learning to become flexible requires that you take a close look at yourself and honestly answer several key questions: What am I like? What are my chief characteristics and traits? If I had to describe myself to someone else so he or she would really understand how I think, behave, respond, and communicate, what would I say? That's an important first step. Improving relationships through flexibility involves understanding who you are.

Similarly, you need seriously to investigate and evaluate the traits of those you want to get along with. How are you alike and how are you different? When you begin to understand the individual differences in the people you relate to, and allow yourself to flex to fit in with those differences, you're on your way to getting along with them. People *want* to relate to those who understand them, who complement them positively, who speak the same language, and who take their unique approaches to life into consideration.

Being Sensitive to Mesh

If you are married, you know there are certain ways of communicating with your spouse that are comfortable for both of you. During these pleasant moments of communication, you *mesh*. There are other times when your relationship is uncomfortable and communication is strained. You feel you are not getting through to your partner and you *clash*. You can probably recognize the same problem in other relationships. Sometimes you mesh with people and sometimes you clash with them. The problem of clashing is often due to thinking inflexibly about the way others respond to life and communicate with you. Clashing means you're not speaking the same language. But when you become sensitive to another person's unique characteristics and take them into account when you respond to him or her, you will mesh instead of clash. When you express sensitivity and flexibility, the other person relaxes, feels understood and accepted, and is more open to you.

I'm the kind of person who wakes up early, bright-eyed, alert, and looking forward to the morning. I can plunge into work and conversations early. And when I meet others who are like I am, everyone gets along great. But not everyone is an early bird. Some people open one eye at a time, with a thirty-minute interval in between. Their brains are at half-speed until they have downed two cups of coffee. By 9:30 A.M. they are functioning and ready to face the day.

If I, feeling bright and chipper, approached such a person at 7:45 A.M. with a list of items to discuss, we would clash instead of mesh. My insensitivity would personify Proverbs 27:14: "If you shout a pleasant greeting to a friend too early in the morning, he will count it as a curse!" (TLB). But if I approached him quietly with just a few words, and kept the atmosphere low-key for awhile, we would mesh. He would be comfortable and appreciate that his uniqueness had been taken into consideration. That's practical sensitivity and flexibility. You *can* learn to adapt to the schedules and energy levels of others in order to get along with them better.

Sometimes you can build a healthy rapport with someone by being flexible enough to adapt the pace of your speech to his. For example, I heard about a man who learned to pace his conversation to that of the people he talked with on the phone in his business. If the caller spoke slowly, he spoke slowly. If the caller spoke rapidly, he did the same. He credited a 30 percent increase in business to his flexibility in pacing his speech.

When you heighten your sensitivity to others, you will notice the uniqueness of others. You will be able to connect on their frequency more readily. The importance of meshing with others was underscored in a study done by a nonprofit research institute. The subjects of the study were twenty-one executives who had been derailed in their climb to the top of the business world by being fired or forced into early retirement. This group was compared with a group of business "arrivers" who made it to the top. Both groups were very similar, but there was one glaring difference: The arrivers were sensitive to the perspectives of others and the failures were not.[1]

I have discovered the same discrepancy in some business people who have come to me for counseling. They were bright, alert, and competent in their fields. But they weren't getting anywhere and some were even sliding down the corporate ladder because they were inflexible with their co-workers. Flexibility can make the difference between success and failure in your relationships. Thankfully, this kind of sensitivity and flexibility to individual differences can be learned.

The human family is filled with variety because each member is different from every other member. We are different in our physical make-up, such as metabolism, neurological structure, and so on. We are different because of family birth order. We are different because of our unique individual life experiences and the patterns of responses which have shaped our personalities. Men are different from women in many ways. For example, women have thousands more nerve connectors between the two sides of the brain than men have. You possess a unique blend of these and many more components, making you different from everyone else.

It is helpful for us to know how we differ so we can be sensitive and flexible to get along with each other. Over the centuries there have been many methods of categorizing people according to differences. Let's explore three of them which will help us to learn and to meaningfully apply flexibility.

Adapting to Different Social Styles

One approach to individual differences which was originally developed to help people build productive work relationships (but which has application in many other areas of relationships) is called *social styles.* This approach categorizes people by external behavior instead of internal motivation. Four social styles describe four major kinds of behavior: *analytical, amiable, expressive,* and *driver.* None is better or worse than another. Each of us tends to have one dominant style.

The *analytical* person combines a high level of emotional control with a low level of assertiveness. These people take a precise, deliberate, and systematic approach to their work. They are data gatherers who evaluate before acting. Analyticals are usually industrious, well-organized, and objective. Think about it: Who are the analyticals in your life? How do you get along with them?

The *amiable* person has a low level of assertiveness and a high level of responsiveness to others. Amiables are sympathetic to the needs of others and able to sense what lies beneath surface behavior. Amiables tend to be empathetic and understanding in their relationships. They have a high level of trust in others. Think about it: Who are the amiables in your life? How do you get along with them?

The *expressive* person tends to be more flamboyant in his behavior. Expressives are high in emotional expression and assertiveness. They like to see the overall picture, run risks to obtain their dreams, and take novel approaches to problem solving. They enjoy life, they have fun, and they can persuade others. They also decide and act quickly. Think about it: Who are the expressives in your life? How do you get along with them?

Drivers have a high degree of assertiveness and a high level of emotional self-control. They know what they want and where they want to go. They are task-oriented and get to the point quickly. They want results. Drivers are pragmatic, decisive, competitive, and independent. Think about it: Who are the drivers in your life? How do you get along with them?

Your dominant social style will not change. But you can learn to exercise the strengths of your subdominant styles and develop flexibility to respond positively to the dominant social styles of others. This is called style *flex*. It's a variation of learning to speak another person's language. Style flex is the activity of accenting the behaviors you have in common with another person. You purposely add to your dominant style other behaviors which will help you mesh with people of other social styles. Style flex also means you subtract some of the natural behaviors of your social style which may prevent another person from relating to you positively. Let's explore how you can flex to get along with the unique characteristics of the four social styles.

Analyticals are left-brain people: factual, skeptical, critical. You can flex to analyticals by giving them time to evaluate situations. When talking with analyticals, identify your subject matter right away. Make sure you are prepared, factual, and logical. They like to hear the pros and cons of all issues, so be ready to present both sides. Converse with them at a moderate pace so they can think about what you say.

Analyticals don't trust overstatements, so avoid exaggeration. If you use words like "never," "always," or "everyone," expect to be challenged. Allow analyticals time to deliberate, but if they are indecisive, don't make the decisions for them. Encourage them to take a stand on the issue. Analyticals respond well to decisions or conclusions that are finalized in writing.

You can flex to the amiable style by being relaxed and by pacing yourself in a moderate fashion. Person-to-person contact is very important to the amiable. Encourage amiables to talk and express their opinions, but don't bore them with small talk. They care for people, so they like to talk about people. When they talk to you, acknowledge that you hear them, but don't offer too much advice. Amiables don't handle pressure too well, so they need to feel that you're walking alongside them, not pushing them. Amiables will usually welcome your help in setting goals and then gently coaxing them to reach those goals. It is important to minimize the risks of decisions or new ventures for amiables since risk is difficult for them. They also need to be able to trust in your assurances to them.

An expressive person can be very enjoyable since you always know what he or she thinks and feels. Expressives enjoy socializing, swapping jokes and stories, and talking about opinions, people, and experiences. You can even talk about yourself with them. If you work with an expressive and need to talk about some business details, begin with a little light, social conversation. Always talk in generalities first—dreams, general feelings, the big picture—and work your way down to details.

Expressives like to take detours and tangents. You may need to keep bringing the conversation back to the main topic. When you reach conclusions or agreements with expressives, be sure to summarize them. You may need to oversee expressives to assure that plans are followed and details are covered.

A driver is a bottom-line person. Be sure to make good use of his or her time. Be specific and clear in what you say—and make your comments short and to the point. Pointless rambling will frustrate the driver and you will lose his or her attention.

A driver tends to be result-oriented, so be sure to focus on goals. Provide options so he or she can make choices. Drivers like to hear the pluses and minuses and the pros and cons of a situation. When you talk with them, they are internally asking, "What's the point of this? What is practical about it? How can I use it now to get results?" Be sure that what you say answers these questions.

Most amiables and expressives tend to be *amplifiers* in conversations, giving lots of information and plenty of descriptive details. Someone has facetiously stated, "When you ask an amplifier for the time, he may give you the history of the modern clock!" When talking with an amplifier, give plenty of details and examples, and expect the same in return.

Conversely, analyticals and drivers tend to be *condensers*, limiting their comments to the essential facts. Lots of details and examples drive condensers up the wall. They want to get to the point. If you usually give an explanation in ten sentences, the condenser will want it in only three or four.

The majority of husbands tend to be condensers while most wives tend to be amplifiers. Wives complain, "He never gives me enough information. I don't want just the headlines; I want the whole story." Meanwhile, many husbands grumble, "I want to bring up a subject and discuss it in two minutes. But she wants to talk it to death for half an hour. So I don't bring it up."

These complaints arise constantly in my counseling office. I challenge every person I see in premarital or marital counseling to flex to fit his spouse's style. And the conflict is so easy to resolve! If the amplifying spouse would just condense a little and the condensing spouse would just amplify a little, each would be more comfortable. It begins with the amplifier saying, "I want to discuss this for seven minutes— total. You can count on me to condense my comments and get to the bottom line." Or the condenser can initiate by saying, "I want to discuss this for longer than I usually do. I promise not to withdraw. I will give you more detail and some feeling words. What time limit for the discussion can we agree upon?"

Adjustments of flexibility like these work. I've seen them work and they can work for you. Condensers can learn to amplify and amplifiers can learn to condense. Expressives and amiables can learn to talk about facts, and analyticals and drivers can learn to talk about feelings. It just takes a commitment to be flexible—and practice.[2]

Adapting to Different Sensory Perceptions

Another way people are different which requires flexibility for getting along is represented by a question I ask at least once a week in counseling: "Does your spouse want to *see* it or *hear* it?" Why do I ask that question? Because each individual perceives life through a dominant sense: seeing, hearing, or feeling. Often people—especially husbands and wives— don't get through to each other because they are appealing to the wrong sense. To get along with people, we need to flex to accommodate the sensory perceptions of others.

A visual person talks about how things look rather than how they sound or feel. For example, most men are visually oriented, primarily experiencing life through their eyes. When a man imagines or remembers, he does so in mental pictures. He prefers face-to-face conversations and meetings instead of telephone conversations. He prefers reading a letter himself instead of having it read to him. He wants to see for himself how a new article of clothing looks instead of having it described to him.

Flexing to relate to visual persons at home, work, or church requires that you approach them through their eyes. Put all verbal communications in writing: notes, letters, memos, etc. Use diagrams. Yes, you can still communicate verbally, but be sure to back up what you say with something the visual person can see. That's why visual aids are so important in teaching. And that's why some spouses don't feel loved by their partners until their spoken words are validated by a love note, card, flower, or something else which is perceived visually.

Even if you are not a visual person, you can learn to communicate with a visual person in terms he or she will understand. You can use terms like, "How does this *look* to you?" or "I *see* what you mean." Does this sound far out? It really isn't. I use these terms all the time to communicate more clearly with the visual person. You can even develop your subdominant senses by becoming aware of your preference and flexing to meet the dominant senses of those around you.

Some people are more hearing oriented, relating more to sounds than to sights. You need to tell these people more than you show them. Auditory people like to talk and to hear others talk. They usually like long conversations, and they are adept both at hearing what is said and what is *not* said. How you speak to them is an important as what you say. As one husband said,"I finally woke up. For years I gave her presents and sent her notes, but these things never seemed to register. But since I started giving her one spoken compliment a day and telling her how much I love her, she's a changed woman!"

Other people are more feeling oriented than seeing or hearing oriented. They crave closeness and love. They are usually more intuitive than logical or analytical in their responses. If you were a car salesman wanting to relate to a feeling-oriented person, you wouldn't say, "Hey, you really look good behind the wheel." Nor would you try to sell a car by saying, "Notice how quietly it rides." Rather, you would say, "Don't you feel comfortable and relaxed in the driver's seat? Wait until you get the sensation of driving this car on the open highway." To get along with feeling-oriented people, you need to flex in order to relate to them through their feelings.

These descriptions have only scratched the surface in the areas of social styles and sensory perceptions. Let me introduce you to some additional resources which will take you deeper into these topics: The book which fully explains social styles is *Social Style/Management Style* (AMACOM), by Robert Bolton and Dorothy G. Bolton. I also described these issues in my book *How to Speak Your Spouse's Language* (Revell), especially in chapters three through nine.

Adapting to Different Personalities

The social styles approach to differences discussed earlier is based upon measurable behavior in individuals. But there are other approaches which not only take into consideration individual behavior, but also the personality behind the behavior. One such approach is the Myers-Briggs Type Indicator. Myers-Briggs is an extremely helpful tool that identifies an individual's lifestyle preferences based on personality. Some of the characteristics we discuss will overlap those presented under social styles. But the focus of Myers-Briggs is personality instead of behavior.

Let me illustrate personality preferences from the physical realm. You were born with a predisposition to be either right-handed or left-handed. As you grew up you preferred your dominant hand for most activities, but learned to use both hands in cooperation. Similarly, you were born with certain personality preferences. As you have grown older, your environment has helped shape the way your preferences are expressed. None of the preferences is wrong, but any preference taken to the extreme can create a personality imbalance. The more you practice your preferences, the stronger they become.

The Myers-Briggs Type Indicator identifies four pairs of preference alternatives. You are either *extrovert* or *introvert*, which describes how you prefer to interact with the world and receive stimulation and energy. You are either *sensing* or *intuitive*, which describes the way you prefer to gather information. You are either *thinking* or *feeling*, which describes your preferences in making decisions. And you are either *judging* or *perceiving*, which describes how you prefer to orient your life to be either structured and organized or spontaneous and adaptive.

Why is it important to understand these personality preferences? Because knowing your type and the types of others around you will help you more fully accept and respond to your spouse, children, parents, relatives, co-workers, employer/employees, and friends. This is no radical claim. Over the years I have seen positive results occur when people took time to understand who they are and who others are. God has called us to get along with people, and this is one tool to help us fulfill that call.

When you are relating to someone whose personality preferences are different than yours, all you need to do to get along is to modify your response a bit. You can learn to use your subdominant characteristics when necessary to help you fit in better. And you can learn not to approach others in ways which provoke them to express their personality preferences in a defensive manner. That's flexibility!

Let me introduce you to just one of the four Myers-Briggs preference alternatives: extrovert/introvert. As you learn how to flex your preference in this area, I hope you will see how easily it can be done in the other three areas as well.

Being an extrovert or an introvert is not a matter of good or bad, right or wrong. Only when a person is too extreme in practicing his or her preference is there danger of an imbalance which can be more hurtful than helpful in relationships. Even when an imbalance occurs, it can be corrected with concentrated effort.

An extrovert's energy tends to increase as he or she interacts with people, while an introvert's energy decreases and drains during sustained interaction with others. Extroverts are charged up by being with people; introverts *need* to be charged up after being with people. Extroverts talk first and think later. Introverts like to rehearse their thoughts before stating them aloud, and wish others would too. You'll hear introverts say, "I need to think about that for awhile" or "Let me get back to you on that."

Extroverts don't mind being interrupted by telephone calls. They can usually do several things at once. They readily share with strangers and they need affirmation from friends and associates about who they are, what they do, and how they look.

Introverts are shy, reserved, and reflective. They have a few close friends with whom they like to share their feelings without interruption. Introverts often keep their thoughts to themselves, while extroverts do much of their thinking out loud: "Now, where did I leave my glasses? Let's see, I had them in the bathroom . . ."

A simple way to determine a person's preference in this area is by listening to his speech. If he speaks loudly and rapidly, overstates his point, repeats himself, and employs a lot of nonverbal communication, you're dealing with an extrovert. But if the person hesitates, thinks before speaking, understates his point, and speaks quietly, you're communicating with an introvert.

In a work setting, extroverts tend to procrastinate when it comes to projects which require silence, introspection, or reflection. They understand the need for this, but put it off in favor of other tasks which they can perform with people. My experience of writing this book is an example of an extrovert trying to activate a subdominant introvert side. I enjoy interaction with people and I have difficulty isolating myself to write. I get up often to walk through the house, take phone calls, visit with my wife, go to the store, and even talk to the dog and cat. These "mini-breaks" help me get through my quiet periods of writing.

Introverts tend to procrastinate when it's time to be with people, such as making a presentation to co-workers or working with a large group. Introverts are usually more content working alone for eight hours without being interrupted by people.

Based on the brief overview of extroverts and introverts above, answer the following questions: Which is your dominant preference? Based on your preference, how do you want others to approach you? How will you approach others with a different preference in order to show that you understand them and are willing to make some adjustments to get along with them?

Let's consider some ways you can respond to those whose preferences are different from yours. When you approach extroverts, give them the freedom to think aloud. Don't assume the statements they make are finished products.

They're merely thinking out loud. Encourage them to brainstorm aloud with you to help clarify their ideas. Realize that extroverts must interact with other people. Try not to limit them from that interaction.

Don't criticize extroverts for trying to juggle several things at once. They can usually do it; invite them to tell you how. Be aware that they may tend to overstate ideas. Ask them for specifics and give them options to choose from. Extroverts who are engaged in a conflict may want to talk through their problems. When they are unable to do this, they may become frustrated. If you can't talk to an extrovert when he or she wants to talk, be sure to set up a time when you will be available to discuss and resolve the problem.

In a marital relationship, an extrovert often demands the spouse's attention and responsiveness. Sometimes this means keeping company without much conversation, but usually an extrovert needs a lot of verbal interaction and reassurance.

How do you respond to introverts? These individuals know they are loved and accepted when they are allowed space and time for quiet. Encourage them to take time to reflect, to think, to sort out ideas, or just to be quiet. If you are an extrovert and your spouse is an introvert, your inclination is to invade your spouse's space. Instead, exercise concentrated effort to allow your loved one the space he or she needs. In return, your spouse may flex a preference for quiet by inviting you to occupy more of his or her space.

Do you remember your school days when part of your grade was based on classroom participation? That was music to the ears of the extroverts, but bad news for the introverts. When the teachers asked questions in class, the introverts were at a disadvantage because the extroverts always responded immediately, even when they didn't have the right answer. Grown-up introverts are still thoughtful and slow about responding to people. So when you discuss something with an introvert, it helps to suggest beforehand, "Here is a topic I would like you to think about and consider before we discuss it." It also helps when you put your idea in writing and allow the introvert to peruse it first before responding.

When there is an interpersonal conflict, introverts need time to reflect and prepare their responses. If you demand,

"Come on; quit stalling. What do you think? I want your answer right now"—forget it. Introverts do not respond well to that kind of pressure. It's better to let an introvert know in advance that he will be called upon for a response, and then help him prepare his response. Say something like, "You always seem to have well-thought-out suggestions. Perhaps you could reflect on this issue and give me your ideas later."

Introverts need to be affirmed for their preference, because often they may feel, "What's wrong with me? Why can't I think on my feet like others?" Reassure them that nothing is wrong. We were all created with unique preferences and the world needs both extroverts and introverts. As we learn to become flexible around those who are different from us, we will convey a strong message of affirmation and acceptance to them.[3]

An excellence resource on the Myers-Briggs Type Indicator is *Type Talk* (Delacorte Press), by Otto Kroeger and Janet M. Thuesen. I have read this book four times, and each time I read it I gain a better understanding of myself and others. I recommend that you read the book, yourself, and discover additional ways for getting along with others who have different personality preferences than you do. (Note: For information on ordering the resources mentioned in this chapter, write to Christian Marriage Enrichment, 1913 E. 17th Street, Suite 118, Santa Ana, CA 92701.)

If learning to flex around others sounds amazingly simple to you, you're right—it is! But are you putting these principles into practice? That's the key. Let's learn from one another's differences and bring balance into our lives. Your family life, work relationships, and friendships can move to a new level of understanding and acceptance as you learn to mesh with others.

8

An Antidote for People-Contamination

Suddenly the red lights began flashing and the warning sirens screeched their piercing alarm. Contamination! Though many safeguards had been devised, tested, and installed, a toxic substance had permeated the atmosphere of the plant. Employees glanced at each other with expressions of concern, then scurried briskly to their security stations. Unfortunately, contamination leaks in the plant were an all too common occurrence. They knew how to cope with the emergency; but that didn't make the experience of surviving the spread of a dangerous toxin less painful.

The containment crew quickly sprang into action to trace the leak to its source. Soon they narrowed their search to one floor of the building. They followed the trail of contamination to an office, opened the door and stepped in. A man at a desk looked up at the crew, smiled, and asked, "What can I do for you?"

"We've been looking for the source of the contamination which is poisoning our company," the crew chief answered. "I think we've found it. We've traced the telltale signs back to you. The poison is criticism. Your critical attitude has contaminated your fellow employees. You have crippled them with discouragement, prevented them from fulfilling their

113

potential, and broken down their morale. The effects of the toxin you spread have been reinforced by many who don't know how to respond to your criticism. But that will no longer be the case.

"The victims of your criticism are learning how to handle the poison so it doesn't hurt them. You may continue to contaminate your co-workers with your critical barbs, but they will still work with you and care for you as a person. They are developing an immunity to the toxin you spread by changing their response to your criticism. You may continue to criticize, but your co-workers have found an antidote which neutralizes the toxin. The power of your critical attitude over them is finally broken."

Far-fetched? Perhaps the story is, but the problem isn't. Many of the people around us nourish us with their positive, uplifting input. Those people are easy to get along with. But others contaminate our relationships with the poison of criticism spread through words which wound us deeply.

These hostile critics come in all shapes, sizes, and varieties. We work with them, go to church with them, and even live with them. You may think that getting along with critical people is conly possible if you eradicate their critical attitudes. If that's your approach you will probably die trying! You can't change everyone. The best way to get along with critical people is to apply the antidote. Learn how to disarm criticism so that it no longer poisons you.

Critics on the Loose

Let me introduce you to several kinds of people who express various forms of destructive criticism. First, there are the *blamers*. They avoid accepting responsibility for their actions by criticizing other people or blaming past experiences which cannot be changed or undone. They are always looking to nail somebody else for "causing" their problems, misfortune, or misbehavior. They say, "This wouldn't have happened if it hadn't been for you. You're the cause of my troubles." They will criticize you for what you did wrong and for what you could have done better. The word "should" is a mainstay in their vocabulary: "You should have known better." "You should have done it my way." "You shouldn't have said that."

Another negative critic is the *hurtful joker*. Humor is a positive method of relating to others. I like to laugh and joke around. If something is funny, even in a serious context, I have difficulty containing my laughter. But hurtful jokers make others the butt of their humor. They specialize in laughing *at* people instead of laughing *with* them. I see this often in husbands or wives who subtly criticize their partners' characteristics, skills, or weaknesses by joking about them in public. A husband says at a dinner party with friends, "My wife serves hamburger for dinner so often that I'm thinking about erecting golden arches in the front yard." Or a wife quips in the couples' Sunday School class, "Gary sings so badly in church that I'm tempted to volunteer for full-time nursery duty at 11:00 A.M. so I don't have to listen to him."

When you confront the joker about his or her stinging humor, the reply often is, "Take it easy. I was just kidding. Can't you take a joke?" This response reminds me of Proverbs 26:18–19: "As a madman who casts firebrands, arrows and death, so is the man who deceives his neighbor and then says, 'Was I not joking?'" (AMP). You know his humor was just camouflage for criticism.

A third kind of critic is the *fault-finder*. This person seems to have an insatiable need to point out others' defects. He is a perfectionist, like those described and explained in the book, *Living With a Perfectionist* (Thomas Nelson), by my friend Dave Stoop. But fault-finders are only interested in revealing the faults of others.

The fault-finder scrutinizes others with a critical eye, especially the more obscure, trivial details of what they say, what they remember, what they do, and what they did in the past. When he spies even the most minor error or deviation from the norm, he is quick to expose it and correct it. He shows off the defects he finds in people as if they were trophies. And do you know what is so maddening about this person? He usually does what he does with a smile, saying, "I'm just trying to be helpful." If it seems you can never please this person, you're right—you can't. Just when you think you've got it all together, the fault-finder comes along to expose your weaknesses and tear you apart.[1]

Another kind of critic at large in the world today is the *cannibal*. These people don't criticize in a joking manner or settle for mere nitpicking. They go for the jugular. They devour family members and co-workers for breakfast, lunch, dinner, and between-meal snacks! They attack through the most severe forms of personal criticism and put downs with complete disregard for the feelings of others.

You've heard their biting remarks: "You've got to be kidding. No one believes that kind of stuff anymore." "A mature person wouldn't get upset over that. Shape up." "What an idiot you are! You made seven mistakes on your spelling test. How could anyone be so stupid?" "Another disaster for dinner. I wish your mother would have taught you how to cook before I married you." "You're late for work again. At least you're consistent." The cannibals are the personification of Proverbs 12:18: "There is one who speaks rashly like the thrusts of the sword" (NASB).

The four types of criticism we have been looking at share the same basic characteristic: destruction. Destructive critics may say they are only interested in remodeling you into a better person by sharing a little constructive criticism. But in reality, the critics described above are not experts in construction, but in demolition. They are intent on putting you down, tearing you down, punishing you, and manipulating you. Their brand of criticism does not nourish; it poisons.

Destructive criticism usually involves the following:

Accusation. Negative critics employ all-encompassing accusatory terms such as "always," "should," "ought," and "never." They say: "You ought to have done better." And, "You are always so sloppy." Or, "You never listen to me." These are real incentives to change, aren't they?

Guilt. A typical critical attack is designed to make the target feel guilty. For example: "I am so disappointed in you. I counted on you and you let me down." "You must not care for me very much or you wouldn't have forgotten my birthday." Parents often use this destructive tool on their children and on each other.

Intimidation. Critics use such intimidating tactics as expressions of impatience and outbursts of anger to convey their disapproval. For example, a man paces the floor fussing and fuming noisily as his wife primps for their evening out. Or an employer stomps through the office shouting angrily, "The next person who takes a two-hour lunch break will be fired!"

Resentment. This form of destructive criticism is often expressed by the person who uses his memory as an ammunition dump. Resentful individuals dig into the past to use your offenses, hasty words, and mistakes as weapons against you. They say things like: "You've been doing this for months." "I remember that nasty remark you made seven years ago." "You're just like your father. He used to treat me the same way." When you don't have a memory as sharp as this person's, you are at a real disadvantage.

Defensiveness Is a Poor Defense

When you are the target of another person's destructive criticism, the natural response is to become defensive. But in reality, the least effective way to respond to criticism is to defend yourself, make excuses, or counterattack. When you are defensive, you place yourself at the mercy of the evaluations and judgments of others. You allow others to dictate who you are, how you will feel, and what you will do. You will react to people instead of respond to them. You will give your critics power over you and you will come out of the situation a loser.

Defensiveness is a barrier that will keep you from getting along with others. But there are great interpersonal benefits to be enjoyed by the nondefensive person. Studies show that married couples develop greater emotional intimacy and bond more readily when there is no defensiveness between them. There are similar benefits in all relationships where defensiveness is replaced by openness.

I know it's difficult not to protect yourself or counterattack the criticism of others, but it is possible to respond in a nondefensive manner. How? Remind yourself that you are responsible to answer to God and to yourself, not to the critical person. Being responsible to God, you look to Him for direction and approval. Being responsible to yourself, you take ownership of your feelings, attitudes, and behavior. If you are aligned with God and with what He wants you to be, you don't need to fear criticism or try to justify your position. You have the power to make your own choices and to grow through the experience of criticism.

As a nondefensive person, you respect and feel good about yourself. You believe in your worth and your capabilities. You possess your own identity and sense of security. Being nondefensive, you can listen to others more objectively and evaluate better what they are saying, even when they express themselves in a negative manner. You can accept the critical person for who he is, even if you don't agree with him. You can accept his right to see the world as he sees it, whether or not it coincides with your view. You're able to relate to him without making disparaging comments or negative judgments about him.[2]

Responding Nondefensively to the Critical Person

Let's consider what you can do when the weapons of criticism open fire on you. The following steps are simple in theory, but they will take effort on your part to implement. If you will reinforce these steps in your mind by reading through them aloud every day for a month, you will be amazed at the changes that will occur in your response to critical people.

Listen to your critics. I realize that I'm beginning to sound like a broken record. But, as I explained in chapter six, listening is an indispensable element for getting along with all kinds of people. Don't tune your critics out. Tune them in by employing the characteristics of a caring listener.

Realize that not all criticism is bad. Consider what God's Word has to say about criticism: "It is a badge of honor to accept valid criticism" (Proverbs 25:12, TLB). "What a shame—yes, how stupid!—to decide before knowing the facts!" (Proverbs 18:13, TLB). "Don't refuse to accept criticism; get all the help you can" (Proverbs 23:12, TLB). "A man who refuses to admit his mistakes can never be successful.

But if he confesses and forsakes them, he gets another chance" (Proverbs 28:13, TLB). Don't automatically assume that all negative criticism is invalid.

Evaluate the criticism for validity. I realize that this step may be easier said than done. Looking for value in the destructive criticism of a blamer, a hurtful joker, a fault-finder, or a cannibal may be like searching for a needle in a haystack. But you must ask yourself, "What can I learn from this experience? Is there a grain of truth in what I am hearing to which I need to respond?" Asking questions like these will shift you from the position of the defendant in a relationship to that of an investigator. Your critic's attack may be grossly exaggerated, unreasonable, and unfair. Disregard the negative statements. Give the critic permission to exaggerate. Eventually the exaggerated statements will blow away like chaff and only the truth will remain. Keep searching for the grain of truth. Try to identify the real cause for his or her critical attack.

Clarify the root problem. Try to determine precisely what your critic thinks you have done, or have not done, that is bothering him or her. It's important that you understand the criticism from the other person's point of view. Ask specific questions such as, "Will you please elaborate on the main point?" or "Can you give me a specific example?" Suppose someone says to you, "You're the most inconsiderate person in the world!" That's a very general statement. Challenge the individual to identify specific ways you have acted inconsiderately. Ask for examples from your relationship with this person. Keep digging until the root is exposed.

Use the checking-listening technique to verify what the critic is saying. Statements which begin "I think you might be saying . . ." or "Are you suggesting that . . ." will help you further clarify the point of contention and move the issue toward resolution.

Think about the charge. There will be times when the process of investigating accusation and criticism may overwhelm you with anger, confusion, or frustration. In the rush of these emotions, your mind may pull a disappearing act—it may go blank! You need time to think before you respond. How can you do this? First I need to warn you against how *not* to do it. Don't ask, "Can I take a minute to think about this?" You don't need to ask anyone's permission to take time to think. Also, don't say, "Are you sure you are seeing this situation accurately?" This question gives your critic the opportunity to make another value judgment on the issue. You are vesting the critic with power he or she doesn't need.

It is better to say, "I'm going to take a few minutes to think this over," or "That's an interesting perspective you have given. I need to think about it." Then ask yourself, "What is the main point my critic is trying to make? What does he or she want to happen as a result of our discussion?" Sometimes it is helpful to clarify that point with the critic by asking, "What would you like to be different about me as a result of our discussion? I'm really interested in knowing."

Respond positively and confidently. Once the central issue has been exposed, confidently explain your actions rather than withering defensively under the attack. I think people who criticize others expect their victims to be defensive, even though these critics sometimes say, "I wish they wouldn't be so defensive when I make a suggestion (their word for a critical demand!)." Critical people say they want their spouses, friends, and co-workers to be nondefensive, but they are often shaken to the core when someone stands up to their criticism.

One man told me that he wished his children wouldn't be defensive. I asked him, "How would you respond if you criticized them and they *weren't* defensive?"

He looked at me, laughed a little, and said, "I guess I'd faint dead away."

I joined him in a chuckle, then I said, "You mean you expect them to be defensive, yet you wish they weren't?"

"Yes," he answered after a thoughtful pause. "I guess that sounds a bit strange. The very thing I want them not to do is what I expect them to do. I wonder if my attitude toward them is helping create their defensiveness."

The affirmative smile on my face answered his inner question better than anything I could have said. We then discussed some new ways he could share his complaints or criticisms with his children so he would be less likely to provoke a defensive response.

Let's listen in on one husband's attempt to respond to his wife's criticism positively and confidently instead of defensively. Sandra is bothered because Jim isn't as sociable as she is. He keeps putting her off when she tries to get him involved with other people. Sandra has a legitimate concern, but Jim also has a legitimate reason for not wanting to be involved, which he has never shared with her. Notice the communication process:

Sandra (quite angry): I'm really fed up. I've asked you time and time again about getting together with other people and you continue to refuse. I'm beginning to believe you don't like people. You're like a hermit. You just sit home and read.
Jim (good naturedly): Am I really that bad? A hermit?
Sandra (with a slight laugh): You're much worse than that. I was giving you the benefit of the doubt.
Jim: Well, can you be more specific?
Sandra: You know when you're being antisocial. It happens at church and it happens when we're with my relatives.
Jim: I'm not sure about that. Can you give me an example?
Sandra: I can give you several. Last week when we were going out for dinner, I suggested that we invite John and Heather to go with us. You were upset because we hadn't planned it out beforehand. You have this thing about planning social activities weeks ahead. I wish you could be more flexible.
Jim: Are you saying that you'd like me to be more flexible? You want me to loosen up and be willing to do things without all that planning?
Sandra: That would sure help. I'd like to see you stop being so rigid. We would both be happier.
Jim: And you thought I was being antisocial the other night because I didn't want to invite John and Heather to join us on the spur of the moment.
Sandra: Yes, but that's just one example. It happens a lot.
Jim: Well, I guess that's something I can work on. I would also enjoy more of a social life, but I need more time to adjust to getting together with others.
Sandra: You've never told me that before. I didn't realize our social activities with others were such a difficulty for you.

Even though Sandra, in her frustration, led off the dialog with an attacking, accusatory statement, Jim didn't let it throw him. And that's the point. You can respond to criticism in a healthy, positive way regardless of the other person's style. Jim responded in such a way that Sandra felt he was hearing her. And Sandra gained a deeper understanding of their personality differences.

Agree with the criticism. No matter how hostile or destructive the criticism may be, agree with it to a certain extent. By doing so you will communicate to your critic that he or she has been heard and that you are not defensive. You can say, "You know, there could be some truth in what you say." You have not admitted to anything, but you are leaving the door open to the possibility. Your response will disarm your attacker and you will no longer have a real opponent.

Offering Constructive Guidance

When you have an opportunity to offer constructive guidance (there's a new term for criticism!), remember not to do so in a negative, destructive, condemning way. Consider the guidelines from God's Word. Jesus said, "Do not judge and criticize and condemn others, so that you may not be judged and criticized and condemned yourselves. For just as you judge and criticize and condemn others you will be judged and criticized and condemned, and in accordance with the measure you deal out to others it will be dealt out again to you" (Matthew 7:1–2, AMP). Paul wrote, "Let us no more criticize and blame and pass judgment on one another, but rather decide and endeavor never to put a stumbling block or an obstacle or a hindrance in the way of a brother" (Romans 14:13, AMP). Our criticism must be that which nourishes relationships, not poisons and contaminates them.

There are many times when we must offer criticism designed to edify and guide. Here are five kinds of criticism to consider: *First,* we need to provide constructive guidance to the people for whom we are responsible in the work environment. If you do not correct sloppy or inaccurate work, you will end up being responsible for a problem. When you affirm and compliment people consistently for their good work, you will find it easier to correct them for their poor work.

Second, if you are a parent, you are responsible to guide, teach, correct, and discipline your children.

Third, you may need to provide constructive guidance to protect the rights of yourself and others. You may find it necessary to confront a loved one concerning irresponsible behavior such as using drugs or alcohol, overeating, or driving recklessly. I have talked to numerous spouses in counseling who were terrified of their partners' driving habits. I have actually asked taxi drivers to slow down because I felt they were driving unsafely.

Fourth, constructive guidance is often needed in the intimate relationship of a marriage. Marriages in which partners never desire a change to occur in each other exist only in storybooks. Learning to live together as husband and wife requires the mutual application of loving constructive criticism over the long haul.

And, *fifth,* there are times in emergency situations when criticism is needed. Often in these crisis moments, constructive guidance is shouted as a command. It's a time for immediate action, not for discussion.[3]

As you prepare to share a complaint or criticism with someone, it is vital that you have gathered all the accurate data on the issue. Ask yourself these three questions: Am I really aware of all the facts? Am I seeing the issue accurately? Is there any way in which I am contributing to this problem or keeping it alive? Also, you must be sure that a similar or worse condition does not exist in your own life (see Matthew 7:3–5). Then offer your constructive guidance using the following steps:

Be brief. Be as concise in your comments as you can be, and be sure to stick to the essentials. Try to limit what you have to say to two sentences. Criticism is often easier for others to receive if you give it in the form of a question with a smile on your face. For example, in confronting a co-worker regarding his procrastination, you might say, "Have you had a chance to get that information I requested last Tuesday?" When the person responds with his intention to complete the task by tomorrow, add, "Great! I'll look for it then. You can leave it in my box."

Be specific. Don't use vague, general remarks. The other person may not be able to decipher your innuendos and get the message. For example, a parent walks into his child's room, looks around with hands on hips, shakes his head in disgust, and says, "I can't believe this place. Where are you hiding the pigs? Can't you be neater?" This criticism is lacking clear constructive guidance.

Put your criticism in plain, positive language. The parent could say, "Jimmy, I would really appreciate it if you would pick up your dirty clothes and put them in the hamper, then hang up your pajamas." Such a clear, specific directive gives the child a greater possibility for a correct response.

Avoid blame and labels. In California, some legislators have tried to institute a no-fault insurance plan. The goal is to shift the focus from "Who's to blame for this accident?" to "What can we do to solve the problem?" In criticism, blaming statements push people's buttons and turn people off. We need a no-fault approach to interpersonal problems, steering away from placing blame and centering on constructive guidance for solving the problem.

When you complain about or correct others, you may be tempted to label them in relation to their offense. You say someone is irresponsible, unreliable, careless, or sloppy. But just because your spouse occasionally forgets to water the house plants doesn't mean he or she deserves to be labeled an irresponsible person. Labels like these are unfair, often hurtful generalizations.

Also, absolute terms like *never, always, every day,* and *every time* are usually inaccurate and should be avoided in criticism. An employee may be late for work three or four times a week, but he's not *always* late. These labels distract from a solution and invite an argument.

In addition to these steps, Dr. Harold Bloomfield gives some excellent suggestions we should follow when we are in the position of sharing constructive guidance:

Make your responses warm and supportive. Share statements like, "I liked what you had to say in answering my criticism. We can talk over some additional suggestions this afternoon. How does that sound to you?" Or consider saying, "I realize that the situation didn't go very well for you. But I am concerned about what we can do together to work it out."

Be patient. Acknowledge to yourself and the other person that it will take time to make any changes in response to your criticism. I share with counselees that the pattern of progress is usually two steps forward and one step backward. I ask counselees to verbalize that changes are difficult but possible. If they walk out with the difficulty of change on their minds, they *will* have difficulty. But if they walk out focusing on the possibilities of change in the midst of the difficulties, they will have hope for change.

Be open to feelings. Acknowledge how the person being criticized must feel by saying something like, "I can appreciate how upset you must feel at this time." Invite the person to share his or her perspective on the problem and listen carefully to what is said. You may ask, "What do you feel might work for you in solving this problem?" or "What do you think we can do about your schoolwork at this point in the semester?"

Guard self-esteem. Some people are overly sensitive to criticism because of their life experiences. So avoid saying anything which would reflect negatively on the other person's character or damage self-esteem. Let the person being criticized know that he or she is valued and cared about, and that you see potential in him or her. Assure the person that the problem and confrontation will not affect your relationship. It may be helpful to say, "Now that we have discussed the situation, it's over with. I won't think about it any more and it won't come between us. Let's go on from here."

Promote cooperation and expectation. A spirit of cooperation and positive expectation on your part will work wonders when you share constructive guidance. Use comments such as, "What can we do together so that we both get what we want?" or "I care for you and want the best for you. I appreciate your listening to me and I think we can both follow through now. What do you think?"[4]

The Upside of Criticism

Sharing criticism, even within the positive framework of constructive guidance, can often be seen as a negative experience. But you can load the experience with positives if you take the right approach. An example of the upside of criticism was described by Dale Carnegie:

> Bob Hoover, a famous test pilot and frequent performer at air shows, was returning to his home in Los Angeles from an air show in San Diego. As described in the magazine *Flight Operations*, at three hundred feet in the air, both engines suddenly stopped. By deft maneuvering he managed to land the plane, but it was badly damaged although nobody was hurt.
>
> Hoover's first act after the emergency landing was to inspect the airplane's fuel. Just as he suspected, the World War II propeller plane he had been flying had been fueled with jet fuel rather than gasoline.
>
> Upon returning to the airport, he asked to see the mechanic who had serviced his plane. The young man was sick with the agony of his mistake. Tears streamed down his face as Hoover approached. He had just caused the loss of a very expensive plane and could have caused the loss of three lives as well.
>
> You can imagine Hoover's anger. One could anticipate the tongue-lashing that this proud and precise pilot would unleash for that carelessness. But Hoover didn't scold the mechanic; he didn't even criticize him. Instead, he put his big arm around the man's shoulder and said, "To show you I'm sure that you'll never do this again, I want you to service my F51 tomorrow."[5]

As the story illustrates, the most important step in sharing criticism is to state the desired behavior instead of complaining about the bad behavior. When you focus on the desired behavior, you are more likely to receive the desired behavior. When you focus on what the person has done wrong, that behavior is more likely to reoccur. For example, if you say, "You never help me pack when we're going on a trip," you're reinforcing the negative behavior. But if you say, "I'd appreciate it if you would help me with the packing when we travel," you have a better chance of getting the response you want.

Be sure to acknowledge in a positive way when your constructive guidance is received by someone. Affirm every small step in the change process. A spoken thank-you or a note of appreciation will go a long way. This is not only a necessary step in keeping criticism positive, it is vital. When you go the extra mile through acknowledgment and affirmation, you will be different and so will the other person. When the efforts of those you correct or guide are noted, they will be more open to change the next time. This is what getting along with people is all about.

Everyone needs to be affirmed several times each day. The need is even greater when criticism is being exchanged. When counseling couples, I often say, "I'm sure that you will feel the need to share concerns and criticisms with each other. That's all right. But for every criticism you share, it will cost you five affirmations during the next few hours after the criticism. And those affirmations must be shared honestly and sincerely, and acknowledged by your partner, before another criticism can be shared." The positive effect of this strategy on a relationship is amazing.

As you reflect on criticizing another person, consider what W. Livingston Larned shared with his son:

FATHER FORGETS

Listen, son: I am saying this as you lie asleep, one little paw crumpled under your cheek and the blond curls stickily wet on your damp forehead. I have stolen into your room alone. Just a few minutes ago, as I sat reading my paper in the library, a stifling wave of remorse swept over me. Guiltily I came to your bedside. These are the things I was thinking, son: I had been cross to you. I scolded you as you were dressing for school because you gave your face merely a dab with a towel. I took you to task for not cleaning your shoes. I called out angrily when you threw some of your things on the floor.

At breakfast I found fault, too. You spilled things. You gulped down your food. You put your elbows on the table. You spread butter too thick on your bread. And as you started off to play and I made for my train, you turned and waved a hand and called, "Good-bye, Daddy!" and I frowned, and said in reply, "Hold your shoulders back!"

Then it began all over again in the late afternoon. As I came up the road I spied you, down on your knees, playing marbles. There were holes in your stockings. I humiliated you before your boyfriends by marching you ahead of me to the house. Stockings were expensive—and if you had to buy them you would be more careful! Imagine that, son, from a father!

Do you remember, later, when I was reading in the library, how you came in timidly, with a sort of hurt look in your eyes? When I glanced up over my paper, impatiently at the interruption, you hesitated at the door. "What is it you want?" I snapped. You said nothing, but ran across in one tempestuous plunge, and threw your arms around my neck and kissed me, and your small arms tightened with an affection that God has set blooming in your heart and which even neglect could not wither. And then you were gone, pattering up the stairs.

Well, son, it was shortly afterwards that my paper slipped from my hands and a terrible sickening fear came over me. What has habit been doing to me? The habit of finding fault, of reprimanding—this was my reward to you for being a boy. It was not that I did not love you; it was that I expected too much of youth. I was measuring you by the yardstick of my own years.

And there was so much that was good and fine and true in your character. The little heart of you was as big as the dawn itself over the wide hills. This was shown by your spontaneous impulse to rush in and kiss me good night. Nothing else matters tonight, son. I have come to your bedside in the darkness and I have knelt there, ashamed!

It is a feeble statement; I know you would not understand these things if I told them to you during your waking hours. But tomorrow I will be a real daddy! I will chum with you, and suffer when you suffer, and laugh when you laugh. I will bite my tongue when impatient words come. I will keep saying as if it were a ritual: "He is nothing but a boy—a little boy!"

I am afraid I have visualized you as a man. Yet as I see you now, son, crumpled and weary in your cot, I see that you are still a baby. Yesterday you were in your mother's arms, your head on her shoulder. I have asked too much, too much.[6]

2

Dealing with Difficult People

It didn't take you many years of living on this earth to discover that some people are more difficult to get along with than others. In fact, some of your family members, co-workers, neighbors, and fellow church members may seem almost impossible to live with. You have probably tried several approaches to dealing with them. You've exhausted yourself trying to change them, only to discover that most of the changes didn't stick and that you needed to change as much as they did. You've tried to accept them as they are, but you only reinforced their impossible behavior and increased your feelings of being victimized or martyred. You've attempted to cope with them, which means to contend with someone on equal terms, but what was equal for you wasn't equal for them. And you've tried to ignore them, but you know that's the last thing God wants you to do.

You have been frustrated because you can't find a way to relate to difficult people without driving yourself crazy or selling yourself short. Well, I have good news for you. It *is* possible for you to relate to the difficult people in your life. I like to call it *positive relating*, which includes elements of acceptance, coping, and responding to problem persons as Jesus Christ did. This approach does not reinforce negative behavior. Rather, it minimizes the difficult person's control over you. Positive relating does not take the behavior of difficult persons as a personal attack. It helps you rise above the conflicts caused by their behavior and allows Jesus Christ to begin a new work in them. Positive relating includes a level of caring for difficult people which can only come through the work of Christ in your own heart and life.

What kinds of people are the most difficult for you to get along with? What kinds of people cause you to feel frustrated, overpowered, torn apart, victimized, set up, confused, frightened, or angry? Chances are, the three types of problem people we are going to discuss in this chapter are the sources of much of your difficulty in getting along with others. We're going to learn how to do some positive relating to negativists, noncommunicators, and controller/dominators.

Dealing Positively with Negativists

Most people generally reflect upon and evaluate thoughtfully new ideas and approaches. Not the negativist. This person is not interested in solving problems or seeking creative alternatives. He or she walks around carrying a bucket of cold water just looking for a place to dump it. The negativist looks pessimistically at most situations, saying, "It's not worth considering. We tried it four years ago and it didn't work then. It will never work."

Negative members have an eroding effect on families, churches, neighborhoods, and businesses. You feel like screaming at them, "Life isn't built on defeat and despair! Why can't you be positive for a change?" But badgering them usually doesn't do any good. In fact, it may even make things worse.

Negativists may not intentionally act the way they do. They often wish they acted differently. But they are afraid to take risks on new ideas. They struggle with disappointments. They don't want to risk failure, so they oppose any opportunity where failure is a possibility. They see themselves as lacking control over their lives, so negativism is their way of expressing control. Unfortunately, the negativists' eagerness to control their own lives leads them to control other people in the process, making them difficult to be around.

How can we get along with these people who seem to spread gloom, despair, and discouragement everywhere they go? Here are a couple of important tips:

Fervently pray for them. The first tip for dealing with the negativists in your life is to cover them with prayer. Pray for them on a regular basis during your daily devotions. Especially pray for them when you know you are going to be with them at work, at church, or at a family gathering. We need to remind ourselves of the tremendous resources which are available to us through prayer. We need to talk to our heavenly Father about these difficult people. We cannot relate to them on our own. We need to see them, their hurts, and their potential through His eyes. We need to remember that God loves these people so much that He sent His Son to die for them.

Praying for the negative person doesn't just mean, "Lord, please change him." Rather you need to ask God to bless this person with His best for him or her. Ask God for the strength you need to relate to this person in a genuine, loving way which does not reinforce or condone the problem.

After your attitude has been refreshed by praying for the negativists in your life, you are ready to interact with them. You may think that the Christian thing to do is to travel the path of least resistance and give in to negativists. But giving in to them only feeds their problems. Jesus called us to feed His sheep, not to feed the sheep's problems. You may want to give in because you often tend to be submissive or to play the victim's role. But giving in to negativists is not the loving thing to do. You must get involved with them in a positive, loving way.

Lovingly interact with them. As you involve yourself with negative people, avoid getting caught up in their arguments. You cannot argue them out of their negativism or motivate them to admit their faults. Their defensiveness and need for control will always spur them to out-argue you, even if their arguments are illogical. You'll never win an argument with a negativist.

I had a seminary student several years ago—I'll call him John—who was a classic negativist. In his own way John controlled those around him, but some of his fellow students had learned how to respond to John lovingly despite his negative attitude.

One day I overheard Randy, one of John's friends, offer a suggestion to a project they were discussing. John responded in his predictable, negative fashion, "It won't work. It's not worth trying."

Randy wasn't fazed by John's negativism and he didn't try to argue with him. Instead he said, "You know, John, that's always a possibility. It might not work. Let's consider that as the first option. Assuming that it doesn't work, what are a couple of other options we could consider?" Randy continued to align himself with John's thought pattern, but kept the focus on the problem instead of John's cold-water approach.

In time they were considering several possible alternatives to the project. As they discussed the options, Randy even voiced some of the negative possibilities for each option himself. As he did, John seemed to relax, apparently encouraged that someone was listening to him, considering his perspective, and still willing to work with him. I was amazed at Randy's skill at interacting with John without reacting to his negativism. Who says a prof can't learn something from his students?

Sometimes, when negativists still won't respond to the kind of loving interaction which Randy displayed, you need to move forward with what you intend to do. But the way you move ahead against the negativist's opposition is vital. Simply discounting their opinions and steamrolling over them will tear down your relationship. You must acknowledge and affirm the person by saying something like, "I have a better understanding of your reasons for thinking the idea won't work, and I appreciate your listening to the other possibilities. But I think I will go ahead with what I originally proposed and give it a try. However, I value your continued perspective as we move along."

The negativist may or may not accept your explanation. But that's not the main issue. After you have tried your best to solicit his or her support, you must move on with what you know to be right, irrespective of the negativist's response. If you measure your success or progress by that response, you again put the control back into his or her hands, thus exacerbating the problem. Lovingly interact with negativists, acknowledge them, and affirm them; but be prepared to move forward without them if they do not join you.

At this point in the interaction process, you must consider the various levels of relationship discussed in chapter one. You need to determine the level of relationship at which you are presently responding and the level you would like to see develop. For example, dealing with a negative spouse, parent, or child will require a deeper level of commitment than dealing with a negative co-worker. If the negativist is a family member or close friend, I recommend that you go one step further with him and seek counseling together.

I have counseled a number of negativists. Often, in the presence of their spouses, I have said to them, "From what I have heard, you are both here for counseling because of one partner's tendency to respond from a negative point of view. You have both indicated that it has become a major problem which is interfering with your relationship. I would like to offer an observation and then make some suggestions. Is that all right?" (I like to ask permission at this stage—which is usually granted—because it allows the client to be part of the next step.)

"My observation is that your negative responses are simply a reflection of a negative pattern of thinking and relating to the world. Just like a computer monitor only displays what is happening inside the computer, your actions and words only reflect what is going on inside your mind. Is this true?" (The response is almost always in the affirmative.)

I continue by explaining how negative thought patterns and self-talk develop. Then I ask, "If there was a possibility of changing your negative view to a positive view, would you be interested in trying it?" Being negativists, some of them are doubtful at first. But I've never yet had anyone turn down my offer.

With the client's permission, I then offer some suggestions and share some helpful resources for turning the negative thinking around. (See chapters eleven and twelve in *How to Speak Your Spouse's Language.*) Then I say, "I want you to try an experiment. Every time you find yourself thinking negatively about a topic or opportunity, start talking about a positive way you can overcome the negative obstacle you're thinking about. Does that sound workable to you? You're probably thinking right now that the experiment won't work, but it's all right if you think that way." The client usually smiles or laughs knowingly at my gentle poke at his or her negativism. My statement is intended to give the client permission to be negative, but since someone else suggested it, he or she will be less inclined to take that option. After a few minutes of discussion, he usually agrees to try the experiment.

Next I direct the client to write out some reminder cards stating his or her objectives for combatting negative thoughts and self-talk. I instruct negativists to read these objectives aloud every morning and evening for the next month until these positive patterns begin to lock into their minds. Then I enlist the support of the spouses by saying, "Since I won't be with you at home this week, would you help your partner by encouraging him and reminding him about our agreement in case there is a lapse?"

Note carefully the specific steps I used in the counseling process above. The negativist can change to a positivist if approached with love and sensitivity. If the negativist in your life is a family member, your vital relationship with him or her will be healthier if you remain patient and affect a change through prayer, interaction, and counseling.

Communicating with the Noncommunicator

People were created to communicate with each other. Unfortunately, some people never got that message. They are the noncommunicators, the silent people, the clams. Have you ever sat in frustration as the seconds and minutes passed while you waited for a response from a noncommunicator? Have you felt your anger slowly build and your muscles grow taut as an apparently indifferent clam shuns you with a blank expression and no eye contact? For the majority of us who enjoy talking and interacting with each other, the clams can be difficult people to get along with.

Noncommunicators are all around us. They are our children, parents, co-workers, and neighbors. Perhaps the most difficult setting for dealing with a clam is in a marriage. After more than twenty-five years of counseling, I have lost track of the large number of silent marital partners who have come through my office. Some of them took a half-hour to answer a simple question from their spouses. Others communicated like they were sending telegrams—as few words as possible to get the message across. Some wouldn't answer their spouses at all—not even with a grunt! Noncommunicators infuriate their partners with the silent treatment.

Why do some people refuse to communicate? I think there are numerous reasons. Some fall silent to control or retaliate against others. Clamming up is an effective way to frustrate a communicative partner. Some use silence to avoid unpleasant or painful interaction or confrontation. Others employ the clam response to avoid facing their own thoughts, fears, and bothersome feelings. When inner issues are verbalized, their reality is more apparent than when you keep a lid on them and guard yourself against them by remaining silent.

I remember my first experience counseling a noncommunicator many years ago. A high school girl came into my office for an hour-long appointment. During that hour she spoke only five times, with periods of silence between her comments lasting more than ten minutes each! I think I counted all the holes in the acoustical ceiling several times during that hour. At the end of the appointment she thanked me and left, apparently feeling better. But I didn't feel better. My first encounter with a clam left me unnerved.

Since then I have discovered that it's okay for someone to be silent. I don't need to fill in all the blank spaces in a conversation. Silence conveys its own message. At the same time I have learned some ways to encourage the noncommunicator to participate more in interaction. You may be thinking, "Why bother with them? If they don't want to talk, forget them." Many of them *want* to talk, but they just don't know how. Our loving approach to noncommunicators is to invite them to talk and to create an atmosphere which will make it easier for them to share their thoughts and feelings.

Again, an indispensable means of encouraging communication with all kinds of people is to show care and concern by being good listeners. Here are some additional steps you can take to help you get along better with the clams in your life.

Accept their silence. Decide in your mind to give noncommunicators permission to be silent and to respond the way they do. This will reduce the pressure and frustration you feel when you expect a response and don't get one. By inwardly accepting their silence you retain a sense of control over the interaction.

Incidentally, the approach of giving people permission to be the way they are can be used to alleviate many frustrating situations. For example, when you are stuck in traffic, consciously give the drivers around you permission to travel with you in the same direction at the same time of day. When waiting in a crowded doctor's office, silently give the doctor permission to spend more time with the other patients, even if it causes him or her to be late for your appointment. By giving an offending person permission for his or her behavior, or by giving yourself permission to experience your unavoidable circumstance, you will tend to relax instead of be upset.

Ask open-ended questions. When talking to a nonresponsive person, avoid asking questions that can be answered yes or no. Use open-ended questions, those which require a full answer. For example, instead of asking, "Did you like the concert?" invite a greater response by asking, "What did you like about the concert?" Another open-ended approach that will draw out the silent individual is to say, "I'm interested in your perception of this issue and I think you have something important to add. Tell me what you're thinking."

Sometimes even when we invite open-ended questions we are greeted with silence. Noncommunicators are not always ready to give more than a yes or no response. One of our tendencies is to "rescue" the quiet person by filling the uncomfortable silence with our own words. Don't feel that you must ease the pressure by elaborating on or illustrating your question or by putting words in the nonresponder's mouth. Instead, consider saying, "I'm interested in what you have to say, but you may need to think about it for awhile. That's fine with me; take your time. When you're ready to talk about it, let me know." Giving permission for silence will take the pressure off both of you.

If the noncommunicator is using his silence as a control tactic, your permissive approach may stimulate him to talk. Why? Because by remaining silent he is yielding control of the situation to you—just what he does not want to do. It's an exercise in reverse psychology. By giving permission for silence you are creating a safe atmosphere and stimulating noncommunicators in a positive way to speak. You're not pressuring them or browbeating them to interact. You are demonstrating that you understand them and are willing to work with them instead of write them off.

Confront silence directly. Another way to invite nonresponders to interact is to address their silence directly. For example, you may say, "Kim, I'm looking for a response from you and you appear to be thinking about something. I'm curious what your silence means at this time." Then wait with an expression of interest on your face, perhaps tilting your head to one side to show that you expect a response.

I have used the following statements effectively in counseling and in day-to-day encounters with noncommunicators as well: "The look on your face tells me that you have something on your mind. I'd like to hear what it is." Or "You may be concerned about how your spouse will respond if you share what's on your mind. I think he's ready to listen." Or "It appears that you're having difficulty speaking right now. Can you tell me why?" "Perhaps your silence reflects a concern about saying something correctly. You can say it any way you'd like."

Once I heard a mother prompt her quiet child to respond by saying, "Johnny, you can tell me what you're thinking out loud or you can whisper it in my ear or you can write it in a note. Which would you like to do?" Her creative approach gave Johnny a choice in the matter—and it usually worked.

A wife used the direct approach with her husband, saying, "Sometimes when I want to talk with you, you seem preoccupied or hesitant. I wonder if it's the topic or if there is something I do that makes it difficult for you to respond. Maybe you could think about it and let me know later." Then she stood up and began to leave the room. But her quiet husband said, "Let's talk now. I'm ready to comment on your last statement."

The direct approach is most successful when we invite noncommunicators to tell us how we have been making interaction difficult for them. But it's so important to listen to them and not allow ourselves to become defensive, no matter what they say. What they share may not be accurate from your perspective, but that's how they see it. Ask clarifying questions at this point to help them gain a more accurate picture of the real problems in your interaction. Be careful not to say anything which might cause them to retreat deeper into their shells.[1]

Controlling the Controller/Dominator

One of the most interesting bumper stickers I've seen on the highway recently read, "Born to Lead." It had a positive tone to it and I liked it. But I know some difficult people who need a similar—but not nearly as complimentary—caption attached to them: "Born to Control and Dominate." I really don't believe these people were born to be so hard to get along with, but they have certainly learned to dominate and override others. I've seen them in all professions. They are easy to notice and hard to ignore. They have an incessant need to be in control of people and situations.

Some controller/dominators are unaware of the extent of their domineering tendencies. Some are more aware, but they exercise control quietly and behind the scenes. Still others are explosive and obvious. Some of the more obnoxious controller/dominators are very competent people, which makes them even more frustrating to be around. We often wish they would fall on their faces just once!

It's difficult to be open and relaxed in the presence of controller/dominators. You're always afraid that what you say in their presence will later be used as ammunition against you. And controlling people usually don't respond openly. Their defenses have been developed to avoid openness. They are skilled at projecting onto others the problems which exist within themselves. The information given by controller/dominators is usually slanted to show that they are right and the rest of the world is off base.

Some controller/dominators are knowledgeable and productive, and others know very little at all. Both can be aggravating. Dominators who are capable—and know it!—will respond to you with arrogant and condescending tones of self-certainty. Their ideas and opinions must win out, and your contributions may be left along the wayside. They don't feel a need to depend on anyone else's information or expertise.

When the dominators' plans succeed, they take the credit. But when their plans fail, they say, "It's not my fault. Someone obviously didn't obey my instructions. The idea was great, but you didn't follow through with it according to plan. Next time, listen to me." I have seen these people dominate a church board meeting. I have seen Christian leaders control their followers this way. I have seen both husbands and wives rule their families in this fashion.

When others resist their dominating tendencies, controllers perceive it as an attack against them and their good ideas. In response, they fall back on an extensive arsenal of weaponry. Anger is a favorite mode of retaliation, either expressed loudly through shouts of irritation and sarcasm, or nonverbally through "the cold shoulder" or "the silent treatment."

I counseled an "all-knowing" controller/dominator who reluctantly made an appointment when one of his interpersonal problems came to a head. As we discussed some of his difficulties, he said, "Norm, one of the problems in my relationships is that I know more than she does. In fact, I know more than most other people. I even know a lot about what you counselors do. I'm not just an expert in one area, but several. That's why I am where I am in my career today. Other people will tell you that I'm an expert. Why shouldn't I tell others what to do when I know more than they know? When a project doesn't work, it's usually because those responsible for carrying through my idea messed up in some way. I like to be sure—and I always am."

Here was a person who had to be absolutely certain of his facts and in complete control of the results. It's very difficult for the controller/dominator to live with uncertainty. To these people, control equals security. They have little tolerance for ineptitude in others, whether it be skill or pace of work.

As we consider how to get along with controller/dominators, we must remember the basic principles for relating to any difficult person: Realize that their behavior is merely a symptom and that God loves them enough to allow Jesus Christ to die for them. And my persistent question to you regarding the dominators in your life is, "Are you praying for them?" What a difference your prayers will make as you take the following steps for getting along with these people!

Don't fight control with resistance. Don't try to fight fire with fire; it won't work. You can't control controllers. Instead, give them permission from your heart and mind to be controller/dominators. Tell yourself it's okay for them to be this way. Assure yourself that you don't need to be intimidated by them, and that you can learn to respond to them in a positive way. Dominators gain a significant amount of their power and control from those who resist them. If you decide not to pull on your end of the rope, there will be no tug-of-war.

Two-thirds of the battle of resistance with dominators is in your mind. You talk with yourself about the dominators and how you feel about them. You focus on their unpleasant behavior and how you wish they would either change or leave. You probably rehearse previous encounters with these persons and anticipate the worst scenario at your next meeting. You keep these negative "instant replays" and "previews of coming attractions" rolling in your mind, and you become physically drained, tense, and anxious as a result. You are so focused on these films of resistance that you are unable to focus on other areas in your life.

If you want to enter the mental film business, create some new films to project in your mind which show you responding in a healthy, affirming, non-intimidating manner to the dominator. See yourself responding calmly to him or her instead of resisting. As you create these mental images, see yourself standing before this person with the arm of Jesus resting on your shoulder, giving you strength. He *is* with you. All too often we forget that fact. We see ourselves entering these conflicts alone, when in reality Christ is with us all the way. Remind yourself of His constant presence.

Realize their insecurity. One of the saddest statements I hear in the counseling office usually comes from a husband or wife who is the victim of a dominating spouse: "It is so peaceful when my husband is gone. The family all gets along so well when he's away. But when he's at home we all tense up waiting for his outbursts. I know I shouldn't say this, but we're happier when he's away. We're tired of being ruled and controlled. That's not the way a family is supposed to live."

The control described by this wife reflects the insecurity which drives her dominating husband. Being right or being in control may have been his method for gaining attention or getting his way as an insecure child. Since it worked so well in his original family, he continues to find security in exerting his control over his wife and children. Keep in mind that the roar of the dominator is usually just a shield covering up a frightened, insecure child.

Lovingly share accurate facts. Since controller/dominators are so dedicated to being correct and precise, you will get along with them better if you speak from an information base which is accurate. Dominators tend to believe that other people don't really know what they're talking about. If they encounter someone who speaks from thorough knowledge and indicates that he or she has done the necessary homework, they may take that person seriously. However, this presentation of accurate information must always be done lovingly and considerately.

Listen, listen, listen. This is a basic step for getting along with all varieties of difficult people. We've talked about listening already and it is thoroughly discussed in chapter six. It takes time and effort, but it will pay rich dividends in your relationships with the controller/dominators in your life. As you listen to the dominator, acknowledge his or her ability and the accurate things he or she says. Affirm this individual even when you are struggling with your own personal feelings about him or her. Often this person is starving for encouragement and affirmation.

Years ago during a counseling case I learned the value of listening to a dominator. When the couple arrived for the first appointment, the woman began talking as soon as I opened the door. As the session went on she interrupted her husband at least fifteen times and tried several times to interrupt and control my interaction with her. My anger began to rise and I felt like telling her off for dominating the session. But I sensed that the Lord was asking me to wait, so I did, realizing that it would do no good to resist her.

As we began the second counseling session a week later, I turned on the tape recorder. About halfway through the session I rewound the tape and played a portion of it as the couple listened. The woman's eyes widened with shock as she realized how often she interrupted and tried to control the conversation. After hearing herself in action, she was ready to talk about her domineering tendencies. She concluded the session by saying, "Thank you for helping me see my problem. I'm sure it won't reoccur as it has."

When the couple returned for a third session, there was a drastic change in the woman. She worked hard to control her interruptions during the session. She really pulled in the reins on her dominant approach. At the end of the session I thanked her and complimented her for containing her interruptions. And was I surprised! This take-charge, headstrong woman had received so little affirmation in her lifetime that she almost didn't know how to handle it. Her tough exterior melted away and her response to my compliments revealed her insecurity and poor self-image. She admitted to me that, if she had not changed, her husband would have divorced her—making him the fifth husband to walk out on her!

I know it's difficult to listen to and care for controller/dominators. They don't appear as if they need it, and they often don't deserve it. But affirmation and caring are commodities which are not given "because of" but "in spite of."

Persist in sharing alternatives. Don't allow controller/dominators to sidetrack you from what you want to say to them. When they interrupt you, come back to what you want to say even if you must start your sentence several times.

This is a variation of the broken-record technique, which involves making the same statement again and again in order to stay in control and get your point across.

When a dominator insists on making a point, acknowledge what he or she says, then offer your alternatives. But remember, the way you share your ideas is very important. I heard one man say in a board meeting, "Bruce, I don't think your way is going to work, so let's look at these other ideas." How do you think that went over with Bruce the dominator?

In a similar setting I heard another man model a positive approach to sharing alternatives with a domineering board member: "There's some real merit in what you've said, George. I'd like us to look at these other two ideas as well, even though we might not end up using them. Looking at them may point out some other possibilities for what you have already presented." Notice how this approach affirmed George while at the same time providing room for introducing alternatives in a positive way.[2]

June, a client of mine a few years ago, shared with me how she learned to introduce alternatives to her controlling and dominating husband:

> For years I was just overwhelmed by him. I cared for him, but his tendency to control me and dominate our social relationships was alienating me from our friends. I have learned to do three things which soften his tendency to control.
>
> First, I ask questions to encourage him to fully explain his controlling actions. One question I always ask is, "What will be the benefits of this action for you and what will be the benefits for me?" That question has stumped him a few times.
>
> Second, I've learned to say, "Jim, you know me. I always like to hear two good ideas instead of one. Give me one good alternative to what you are suggesting that we do." Now and then he actually comes up with two workable alternatives.
>
> Third, I request a delay in Jim's decision-making. I simply say, "I would like some time to think this over." I know it frustrates him at times, but he's learned that I can't be hurried into a decision. He knows I need time to sort through his argument and he is more willing to give me the time I need.

I'm sure you have your own list of difficult people to deal with which go beyond the descriptions in this chapter. There are many variations of problem people around us. You can avoid many of them at church, at work, or at the health club. But there are many others you cannot avoid. In the main, your calling is not to be an avoider, but to be a relater. Instead of avoiding the difficult people in your life, try again to relate to them using the guidelines in this chapter. But this time don't do it alone. Relate to these people out of the resources you find in Jesus Christ. Claim His presence in your life and in all your relationships.

10

Relatives:
The Ultimate Challenge!

John sat in the counseling office telling me his story. "It's ridiculous! My wife Sally and I get along fine for months at a time. Then her parents come to visit us for two weeks and our entire relationship turns upside down. It's so difficult to relate to her parents. They just sit around not wanting to do anything. They don't talk much, but they stay on and on. I get edgy and irritable, and Sally and I end up fighting over unimportant issues." I nodded understandingly. I've heard stories like John's from numerous couples and individuals.

"It's no better when my parents visit," he continued. "My mother walks in and takes over the house, provoking instant conflict between Mom and Sally. Mom wears her feelings on her sleeve, takes things so personally, and pouts when she gets hurt, driving Sally and me up the wall. There's got to be a better way to handle our relationships with our parents."

Getting along with relatives and in-laws is a challenge almost from the moment boy meets girl. Different family customs, traditions, and lifestyles can become sources of conflict for a newly married couple. Young husbands and wives argue over simple issues like whether ham or turkey is served for Easter dinner, or whether gifts are opened Christmas Eve or Christmas day. Past traditions and present expectations can also turn vacations into a source of family conflict. He grew up visiting relatives during vacations, but she is accustomed to vacationing in the mountains or at the beach to get away from relatives. Vacation questions such as where to go, who to visit, what to do, and how long to stay become the kindling for roaring family feuds.

Push/pull conflicts are also common between grown children and their parents. A young husband is tempted to accept a job in a distant city. But his wife's parents want the couple to stay put. "We won't see you as often," they argue. "We'll miss the grandchildren and they will miss us, and we can't travel well enough to come see them." How can families get along in situations like this?

Kate and Phil came for counseling because they were not getting along with their parents. "Phil's mother is our problem," Kate said. "I can get along with just about anyone, but I have so much trouble with that woman. She still has Phil tightly tied up in her apron strings. I tried to be nice to her when we were first married, but she has never liked me. She didn't believe I was the right woman for her son. She spoiled him, but I won't wait on him hand and foot like she did."

"Kate is just jealous of my mother," Phil interjected. "She doesn't even want our kids to have gifts from Mom. I think Kate should at least try to understand how Mom feels now that her husband and only son are gone. If Kate would treat Mom lovingly and decently, most of the problems between them would be cleared up." Have you heard about, or personally experienced, family problems like these?

When family members work together in a business arrangement, they may have problems getting along. When parents move in with their adult children, or when grown children move back in with their parents, they may have problems getting along. When an only child marries someone from a large "tribe," the families may have problems getting along. The conflicts we experience within families are the same kinds we experience with nonrelatives, except that family conflicts are often deeper. Why? There are several reasons. We hold higher expectations for family members, so disappointment and conflict come easier. The quality of attachment between family members is greater, so dissension is felt more deeply. Family values are often deeply rooted, causing any deviation from family tradition to be seen as disrespect. Wherever positive feelings are intense, as they are in a family, negative feelings will often be equally as intense.

It is more important for family members to learn to get along with each other than for other relationships. Why? Because in work relationships, friendships, and even dating relationships, if problems become too great or adjustments too difficult, you can terminate the relationship. But you can't resign from being a parent, child, or in-law. Problems must be dealt with in family relationships because you can't walk away from your family.

I suppose we all have relatives from whom, if we weren't tied to them by blood or marriage, we might walk away. But family commitments and obligations are deep and lasting. We must learn to get along with our relatives at all costs.

How Do You Relate to Your Relatives?

In chapter one we discussed several different levels of relationships. These various levels of relating to people also apply with our relatives and in-laws. We have both binding and casual relationships with family members. In fact, you may have some relatives that you see only once or twice in five years. It's a casual family relationship and it's not a problem. It's those binding family relationships with relatives we see on a regular basis that create the greatest amount of tension.

Relationships with family members can also be categorized as minimal, moderate, strong, and quality. You may want to review these categories in chapter one as you apply them to relatives and in-laws.

Think about the people you are related to by blood or marriage: your parents, stepparents, siblings, children, stepchildren, grandparents, in-laws, aunts, uncles, cousins, nieces, nephews, etc. With whom do you have a casual relationship? With whom is your relationship more binding? With whom do you get along best? With whom is it difficult for you to get along? What are the reasons you get along well with some but not with others? With whom is your relationship minimal? moderate? strong? quality?

The following exercises will help you evaluate and identify the levels of relationship you presently experience with your relatives and in-laws. Take a sheet of blank paper and number from 1 to 15 down the left margin. Across the top of the paper write the four words *minimal, moderate, strong,* and *quality,* as in the Relative Relationships Inventory example.

Relative Relationships Inventory

Name	Minimal	Moderate	Strong	Quality
1.				
2.				
3.				
4.				
5.				
6.				
7.				
8.				
9.				
10.				
11.				
12.				
13.				
14.				
15.				

Beside the numbers write the names of the fifteen relatives and in-laws with whom you have the greatest contact. Check the quality of the relationship you have with each person: minimal, moderate, quality, or strong. Then, using a different mark, indicate the level of relationship you want to achieve with each person in the future. As you review the marks on the sheet, you will realize that you have relatives you truly love, some you only like, and others you don't like at all! The difference between the two marks, if any, will show you the amount of work ahead of you for improving each relationship.

Let's take the evaluation one step farther. Which of your relatives is the most difficult for you get get along with? Perhaps answering the following questions will help you determine the reasons for your problems:

1. Do you live with or near this person? Why?

2. How do you feel about the amount of personal or telephone contact you have with this person? How would you like the amount of contact to change?

3. How would this person describe your relationship to someone else?

4. How would this person describe you to someone else?

5. Do you avoid this person in any way? If so, how?

6. When do you get together with this person? Is it pleasant? If so, why? If not, why?

7. How does this person respond when you do something you want to do rather than what he advised you to do?

8. How do you respond when this person does what he wants to do instead of what you advise him to do?

9. Do you need this person's approval? If so, why? How do you try to gain approval from this person?

10. Do you get together with this person at significant family gatherings such as birthdays, anniversaries, holidays, etc.? If so, what are these times like? How would you like them to be different?

A very common family problem involves adult children leaving home to live on their own and parents releasing them to do so. I know. Our daughter was recently married, leaving our home at age twenty-seven. Since the age of nineteen, she had moved and returned on three different occasions. It is difficult for some parents to release their adult children. When parents continue to give unsolicited advice or interfere in other ways as their adult children leave home, feelings of anger may arise. And when this occurs, the child's choice seems to be either to stifle his or her anger or let it out. These are the two alternatives most people select. But there is one other option: propose an effective solution to the problem. In fact, this should be the main goal in any difficult relationship.

Kent was a thirty-two-year-old man who had lived with his parents until he was married at age thirty. Two years after the wedding, Kent and his wife June came into my office. A strain was developing between them. The problem was Kent's mother, who was continually interfering in his life. Incidentally, many people think that most in-law problems occur between the husband and his wife's mother. But that's not the case. In most instances, in-law conflicts arise between the wife and her husband's mother, as in Kent's situation.

Kent's mother phoned him or visited him often to badger Kent and June with uncalled-for advice. Kent tended to ignore what she said, only to steam with anger after she left. He refused to confront the problem head on.

After listening to Kent and June tell their story, I looked at Kent and said, "Is the way you are handling this problem with your mother working?"

"No," he answered dejectedly.

"Then you will lose nothing by trying a new approach, will you?" I challenged.

"You're right, Norm," Kent agreed. "I've got nothing to lose and something must be done. I really love my wife and my parents, but I feel caught in the middle. I know Mom's intentions are basically good most of the time. Perhaps I contributed to the problem by not moving away from home sooner. Now I've got to handle this situation."

I offered a suggestion that was not original, but which has proved quite effective for most problems like Kent's. It required that Kent take a new approach to the problem. He didn't have to wait long to try out his new plan.

The next week Kent's mother called him at home and gave some suggestions for his vacation. He listened to her patiently, then said, "Mom, I need to share something with you. I become a bit upset when you make so many suggestions on what June and I should do. I realize that you love us and want the best for us. And I love you, too. Now that I'm on my own and married, I need my independence. I enjoy some of our interaction, but too many suggestions bother me. I would like you to do something for me. I think it would work better if I called you once a week and you called me once a week. We can share what's going on in our lives. If you have a suggestion, please ask me first if I would like to hear your ideas on that subject. I think this way we will enjoy the relationship better."

Kent had prepared himself for several possible ways his mother might respond to this initial conversation. She could sound hurt and taken aback. She could state defensively that she was just trying to be helpful. She could withdraw by not calling for a week or two. Or she could respond with statements of self-pity. Kent's mother did them all. But, in time, the relationship became much better. Kent had to repeat his request on two subsequent calls before it "took" with his mother. But it began to work.[1]

Do you have any relatives who respond in this way? If so, how does it affect you? How do you respond? As in Kent and June's case, there may be times when you need to sit down with an objective third party to discuss problems with relatives or in-laws. The neutral observer may be able to point out previously unseen ways of solving the problem. Often role-playing a potentially troublesome confrontation can ease much of your discomfort. It allows you the opportunity to walk through the event in a safe environment and practice responding in advance of the actual encounter.

The High Cost of Not Relating

I have had people say to me during counseling, "Now that I'm an adult, I thought life would be different. I assumed that I would not have to deal with family tensions any longer. I don't want to be involved with some of my irritating relatives. In fact, I would be happy never to see some of them again."

Have you ever felt like this? Of course, as an adult you can ignore the family members whom you find it difficult to relate to. But there is a price to pay for avoiding relationships with relatives or in-laws. You may want to evaluate the cost to yourself and others before deciding not to resolve family conflicts.

First, by failing to put to rest issues of family conflict, you may experience recurring anger and tension every time you contact that person. Furthermore, your negative feelings will usually spill over onto other family members, complicating the problem.

Second, unresolved conflicts could cause you to dread family get-togethers or reunions for years to come. Many people joyfully anticipate being with their families and spend months planning for those few occasions. But if you have unresolved conflicts, your anticipation for these events is anything but joyful. You are on pins and needles. Your anxiety builds as the date draws nearer. Then you wear a plastic smile to get through it, while your insides churn. Is not getting along worth this kind of tension?

Third, there's the guilt. For example, there are many people today who are filled with guilt and regret because they failed to resolve their conflicts with relatives who died unexpectedly. Why wait to clear up problems until it is too late? I've talked to many people who said, "I'm so glad I reached out to that person when I did. If I had waited another week it would have been too late." One person told me, "I feel so much better having worked through my relationship with my stepfather to a positive level. I was saddened when he was killed in an accident, but I knew that the air was clear between us and I have no regrets." Will you be able to say this about your problem relationships?

A fourth major difficulty with choosing to ignore problem relationships is the effect it could have on your children. Some adults who will not relate to family members deny their children the opportunity to relate to their extended family. Restricting a child's relationship with family members may rob him or her of the enjoyment of valuable interaction with aunts, uncles, cousins, grandparents, etc.

Fifth, unresolved family conflicts lead to overreactions and self-fulfilling prophecies. You become supersensitive to the problem relative to the point that you tend to read into his comments and responses meanings which are false. You may even begin responding negatively to anyone who reminds you of this person, dumping anger and bitterness on unsuspecting and undeserving people.

Last, perpetuating unresolved relationships means that you will carry an excessive emotional load and labor under unnecessary anxiety. You know that this person is a part of your life—whether or not you like it. And you carry with you the image of what the relationship should be or could be, but is not. The tension between the two creates an emotional burden that will cause you difficulty until the conflict relationship is resolved.[2]

How Not to Resolve Family Conflicts

It should be obvious to you that an important element in getting along with relatives and in-laws is resolving family conflicts. Before talking about ways to solve family relationship problems, I want to share with you some ways which do *not* work. I have enjoyed reading the suggestions which Dr. Leonard Felder guarantees will make a relationship worse instead of better.

First, there is the *Frozen Smile* approach. This technique is straight out of the ice age! You sit with your relatives at a family gathering, forcing a smile to cover your negative emotions about being in the same room as your feisty old Aunt Gertrude. Behind your frozen smile you want to scream at her. You sit calmly, but inside you're thinking you would rather be anywhere else. You try to fool your family and yourself with your calm-looking exterior, but does your act really solve anything?

Then there's the *Reform School* approach, by which we attempt to reform some of the irritating relatives we must relate to. We give them advice to correct their behavior, which we hope they will both hear and heed. But how often have you seen this approach work? It seems whenever we approach relatives with some constructive criticism, they know what's coming and they put their minds on hold so nothing penetrates.

How often have your relatives tried to reform you? You can defuse these encounters in a positive way. One man told me, "The last time I saw my pushy uncle, I knew he wanted to harp on me like he always does. So I started the conversation by telling him everything I knew he was going to say to me. Then I said in a pleasant tone of voice, 'If that's what you were going to tell me, Uncle Bill, you can see that I already know it. I haven't followed that advice in the past, so I don't need to hear it again. Since we've settled that issue, what else would you like to talk about?' He didn't know what to say next, but we ended up having one of the best conversations we've ever had. I think he respected me more after that. He began to treat me as an adult instead of his little nephew."

Some people employ the *Distraction* approach in family relationships to avoid interaction with relatives they don't like. For example, a common distraction used to avoid conflicts at a family gathering is to gorge yourself on food. You either hide out in the kitchen eating or, at meal time, occupy yourself consuming great quantities of food. Eating makes you feel better and keeps your mouth busy, giving you an excuse not to talk. This approach may work for awhile, but soon your stomach rebels and you realize that nothing positive was accomplished.

Another wrong approach to family conflict is the *Excuse Search* approach. This person is just looking for another excuse to lambaste an irritating relative. Cousin Clyde thinks, "If Cousin Charlie brings up that subject one more time, I'm going to tell him just how I really feel." And what happens? Charlie *does* bring it up again because Clyde is consciously or subconsciously directing the conversation back to the topic in order to lay into Charlie. Clyde has the excuse he wants for rekindling a family fracas, and he often comes away looking like an innocent victim.

Some family members use the *Sacrificial Lamb* approach to conflicts. These people appear to make sacrifice after sacrifice for another family member. But they hold a hidden agenda. They give of themselves to elicit guilt in the other person to get what they want out of the relationship.

Finally, there's the *It Doesn't Hurt* approach. Probably the most common mistake family members make is denying the hurt they feel in the relationship. But despite the denial, the emotional wounds remain raw and festered. When you bury your hurts instead of exposing them, you bury them alive, and they will resurface in other unpleasant ways. For example, many cases of obesity are directly related to family anger that has never been resolved. Overeating is an attempt to cover or block the inner pain. Hypertension and stress are also symptoms of buried hurt.[3]

Can you identify with any of the nonproductive approaches to family conflict as you compare them to the list of relatives you evaluated earlier in this chapter? Have you been guilty of complicating family relationships by employing these approaches yourself?

Positive Steps toward Positive Relationships

Coming up with effective solutions to family conflicts involves taking charge of the situation instead of letting the situation control you. Here are ten positive steps you can take to help turn your negative family relationships into positive ones:

1. *Apply previous suggestions.* Remember: Every suggestion given in this book for getting along with people applies to family members as well as co-workers, friends, neighbors, etc. You may want to reread the previous chapters with the names of problem family members specifically in mind. Consider how you can apply the principles already discussed in your troublesome family relationship.

For example, in chapter one empathy was suggested as a major characteristic of positive relationships. In relating to family members, personal values, standards, and expectations often become the basis for conflict. Each person attempts to foist his own values, standards, and expectations on other family members. We often bristle and chafe when relatives crowd us with opinions that differ from ours. You can blame or attack them for their opinions, or exercise empathy by discovering what lies behind their opinions. If you had the same background or life experiences, you might end up with the same opinions. That's empathy: seeing life through their perspective.

You don't need to agree with your relatives' opinions, but you can at least give them the courtesy of listening to them and understanding their perspective. You can also learn to explain your perspective calmly while demonstrating love and respect for them and their opinions.

2. *Identify expectations.* You not only need to identify the expectations you hold for other family members, but identify the expectations they hold for you. Whether we

realize it or not, everyone operates with lists of expectations. This is why I advise ministers who are candidates for church staff positions to request church board members to supply a list of expectations they have for the minister and his wife. Then I suggest that the minister supply the board with a list of his expectations for the church. Specific lists help dispel myths before they grow into major disappointments and problems.

In family relationships, expectations often fall into the categories of who people should be and what they should do. Problems occur because family members are not living up to each other's expectations. What's more, everyone is tired of trying to do so. Unmet expectations lead to anger and resentment. Unmet expectations harden into demands which, when resisted (as they almost always are!), unleash a barrage of negative feelings and reactions.

When someone doesn't fulfil your expectations, you view that person as being in the wrong. At the same time, he probably sees you as being in the wrong. And the more you try to prove each other wrong, the more you will respond by trying to prove yourselves right. Family conflicts like these have been going on for thousands of years. Don't think you will escape them if you fail to identify the expectations involved.

3. *Clarify what you want in the relationship.* If you completed the exercise earlier in this chapter, you have identified your family relationships as casual or binding, minimal, moderate, strong, or quality in nature. The second step—deciding where you want the relationship to go—is equally important. Deciding what you want the relationship to become establishes your path for growth. Be aware that you must be ready to take the initial step to see this growth happen. Waiting for the other person to lead places you under his control. He may never take the first step, but you can.

4. *Focus on the good times.* Spend some time thinking about occasions in your life when your relationships with irritating family members were pleasant. Determine what made those occasions pleasant and what you can do to recapture those qualities.

5. *Get better acquainted.* How much do you know about your problem relatives' life and background? What events contributed to their being the way they are today? What can you do to find out more about them and their past? I know some people who have sat down with their relatives to discuss individual and family history. Others have leafed through a family photo album with a relative as a means for asking questions about background.

6. *Discover reasons for criticism.* If the other family member has been interfering in your life for some time, or is constantly critical toward you, investigate why you have allowed him or her to continue to do that. Perhaps you are relating to the person as a parent or a child instead of a peer.

7. *Explore your feelings.* Make a list of all your feelings toward this person. Then indicate which feelings you want to keep and which you would like to put away. List the positive feelings you would like to develop which didn't appear on your first list. Determine what you will need to do to eradicate your bad feelings and nurture your good feelings.

It is best not to carry inside a load of anger or resentment toward a difficult family member. For example, if you experience an unpleasant encounter with a relative that leaves you feeling angry, immediately write a letter to this person—a letter you will not mail. In the letter describe all the feelings you presently have, the feelings you would like to have, the type of relationship you think is possible, and how you will pray for this person during the next week. Sit down alone facing an empty chair and read the letter aloud as if your relative were sitting there listening. Then destroy the letter. You will find that releasing your anger in this way allows you to continue with life without unnecessary emotional baggage.

8. *Forgive others.* If you have been offended by a family member, forgive him. You may say, "But Norm, if you only knew . . ." Yes, I'm sure you may have been deeply hurt. But allowing those hurts to live inside you through unforgiveness hurts you even more deeply. Make a list of the benefits of forgiveness and unforgiveness, then compare lists. If you need assistance with the step of forgiving

others, I recommend the book *Forgive and Forget* (Harper and Row), by Lewis Smedes, as a helpful resource.

9. *Introduce new alternatives.* When you get together with your relatives, can you predict what will be said, what is going to happen, what foods will be served, etc.? No wonder families don't get along. Often our family traditions are so predictable that people are bored, and boredom leads to irritation and conflict.

I know what that's like. For twenty-seven years our family Thanksgiving dinners were fairly predictable, always served in one of our homes in Southern California. But recently we tried something different. Joyce and I took our mothers with us to a cabin in the mountains and spent the night, celebrating Thanksgiving there. Other relatives dropped in during the weekend and we had a wonderful time.

What can you do differently to introduce zest to your family gatherings? Some families have potluck suppers when they get together so no one is stuck cooking a big meal for everyone. Some families meet at restaurants and leave the cooking and cleanup to someone else.

What about those boring family conversations? Sometimes invoking a "gag rule" on an over-talked subject will allow for new topics to be introduced and discussed. One family began the tradition of each member introducing a topic for conversation which the family had never talked about before. Their family gatherings are now rich and enjoyable, anticipated instead of dreaded.

10. *Anticipate changes for the better.* It is possible for your family relationships to get better. The changes may not happen in the relatives you have trouble with, but that's all right. Changes in you will be sufficient. Maintain an attitude that it is possible for all of you to change.

I've heard so many reasons why a family relationship will never change:

"But Norm, I really have tried everything."

"But Norm, you don't know this person. He is so stubborn."

"But Norm, how can I get along with my aunt when no one else can?"

"But Norm, it's not worth the effort. I'll just continue to avoid him."

"But Norm, she's been this way for sixty-eight years. Do you really think she'll change?"

When you expect people to stay the same, and when you expect yourself to stay the same, your expectations will be fulfilled. It's so easy to focus on the negatives in others. Instead, we need to see them as God sees them. Every negative trait, quirk, or liability has a positive side. You need to become a talent scout who looks for the strengths and undeveloped potential in your family members. Your calling in difficult family relationships is not to contribute to the problem, but to contribute to the solution.

Above all, be an encourager in your family. Paul wrote: "Encourage one another and build each other up" (1 Thessalonians 5:11, NIV). What better place to apply this verse than among your relatives and in-laws! You can change yourself. You can change your family relationships.

I love the Old Testament story of Caleb and Joshua. Twelve spies were sent into the Promised Land, and when they returned they gave a conflicting report. As Chuck Swindoll says, "Ten saw the problem; two saw the solution. Ten saw the obstacles; two saw the answers. Ten were impressed with the size of the men; two were impressed with the size of their God. Ten focused on what could not be accomplished; two focused on what could easily be accomplished by the power of God."[4]

Perhaps there are times when we feel like the ten doubters when it comes to believing that we can get along with people. But the response of Caleb and Joshua works for us as we view our relationships just as it worked for them as they viewed the Promised Land. Give yourselves and others the benefit of the doubt. Withdrawal in fear accomplishes nothing. Facing the issues and obstacles of relationships is the only way to grow in them.

And, thank God, we don't need to do it under our own power. Let God lead you and empower you in your relationships and you'll see how easy it can be to get along with almost anyone.

Notes

Chapter 1

1. Myron Rush, *Hope for Hurting Relationships* (Wheaton, IL: Victor Books, 1989), adapted from p. 29.
2. Carol C. Flax and Earl Ubell, *Mother, Father, You* (Ridgefield, CT: Wyden Books, 1980), adapted from pp. 192–201.
3. Rush, *Hope for Hurting Relationships*, p. 21.
4. Leo Buscaglia, *Loving Each Other* (New York: Holt, Reinhart and Winston, 1984), p. 15.
5. Dale Carnegie, *How to Win Friends and Influence People* (New York: Pocket Books, 1936), adapted from pp. 55–56.
6. Charles Swindoll, *The Quest for Character* (Portland, OR: Multnomah Press, 1988), adapted from p. 67.
7. Margery Williams, *The Velveteen Rabbit* (New York: Avon, 1975), pp. 17–18.
8. Charles Swindoll, *Improving Your Serve* (Waco, TX: Word Books, 1981), pp. 116–117.
9. Alan Loy McGinnis, *The Friendship Factor* (Minneapolis, MN: Augsburg, 1979), adapted from pp. 36–37.
10. Lorraine Hansberry, *Raisin in the Sun* (New York: Signet Books, 1959), p. 121.
11. Robert Bolton, *People Skills* (Englewood Cliffs, NJ: Prentice-Hall, Inc., 1979), adapted from pp. 259–272.

Chapter 2

1. J.I. Packer, *Knowing God* (Downers Grove, IL: InterVarsity Press, 1973), p. 37.

2. David Seamands, *Healing Grace,* (Wheaton, IL: Victor Books, 1988), p. 142.

3. Harold Bloomfield and Leonard Felder, *Making Peace with Yourself* (New York: Ballantine Books, 1985), adapted from pp. 1–8.

4. Lloyd John Ogilvie, *Discovering God's Will in Your Life* (Eugene, OR: Harvest House Publishers, 1982), pp. 144–145. Used by permission.

5. H. Norman Wright, *Uncovering Your Hidden Fears* (Wheaton, IL: Tyndale House Publishers, 1989), adapted from chapters 1–2.

6. Dr. Sidney Simon, *Getting Unstuck* (New York: Warner Books, 1988), adapted from pp. 236–240.

7. David Burns, *Feeling Good* (New York: Signet Books, 1980), pp. 325–326.

8. Alan Loy McGinnis, *Bringing Out the Best in People* (Minneapolis, MN: Augsburg Publishing House, 1985), adapted from pp. 71–72.

9. Herman Gockel, *Answer to Anxiety* (St. Louis, MO: Concordia Publishing House, 1961), no page number in original source.

10. William and Kristi Gaultiere, *Mistaken Identity* (Old Tappan, NJ: Fleming H. Revell, 1989), adapted from pp. 94–95.

11. Charles Swindoll, *Living above the Level of Mediocrity* (Waco, TX: Word Books, 1987), p. 29.

12. Ibid., p. 26.

Chapter 3

1. Michael E. McGill, *Changing Him, Changing Her* (New York: Simon and Schuster, 1982), adapted from pp. 29–38.

2. Ibid., p. 257.

3. Ernie Larsen, *Stage II Recovery* (San Francisco: Harper and Row, 1987), adapted from pp. 34–37.

Chapter 4

1. Ernie Larsen, *Stage II Relationships* (San Francisco: Harper and Row, 1987), p. 34.

2. Alan Loy McGinnis, *Bringing Out the Best in People* (Minneapolis, MN: Augsburg Publishing House, 1985), adapted from p. 29.

3. Larsen, *Stage II Relationships,* pp. 54–55.

4. Ibid., adapted from pp. 34–40.

5. Anthony Campolo, *Who Switched the Price Tags?* (Waco, TX: Word Books, 1986), pp. 69–72.

6. Carmen Renee Berry, *When Helping You Is Hurting Me* (San Francisco: Harper and Row, 1988), p. 45.
7. Ibid., adapted from pp. 42–47, 57–60.
8. Joseph Bayly, *Psalms of My Life* (Elgin, IL: David C. Cook Publishing Co., 1969), pp. 40–41. Used by permission.

Chapter 5

1. Gene Getz, *Living for Others When You'd Rather Live for Yourself* (Ventura, CA: Regal Books, 1985), p. 21.
2. Robert Anthony, *Super Persuasion* (New York: Berkley Books, 1973), adapted from pp. 45–48.
3. Robert Conklin, *How to Get People to Do Things* (New York: Ballantine Books, 1979), adapted from pp. 113–115.
4. Ibid., adapted from pp. 34–40.

Chapter 6

1. Dale Carnegie, *How to Win Friends and Influence People* (New York: Pocket Books, 1936), adapted from p. 92.
2. Carol C. Flax and Earl Ubell, *Mother, Father, You* (Ridgefield, CT: Wyden Books, 1980), adapted from pp. 43–55.
3. Aaron T. Beck, *Love Is Never Enough* (New York: Harper and Row, 1988), adapted from pp. 74–75.
4. Christopher News Notes, Number 195, mimeogaphed.

Chapter 7

1. Robert Bolton and Dorothy G. Bolton, *Social Style/Management Style* (New York: AMACOM, 1984), adapted from p. 11.
2. Ibid., adapted from pp. 20–24, 33.
3. Otto Kroeger and Janet M. Thuesen, *Type Talk* (New York: Delacorte Press, 1988), adapted from chapters 3–6.

Chapter 8

1. Jerry Greenwald, *Be the Person You Were Meant to Be* (New York: Dell Publishing Co., 1979), adapted from pp. 224–226.
2. Theodora Wells, *Keeping Your Cool Under Fire* (New York: McGraw-Hill Book Co., 1979), adapted from pp. 44–50.
3. Robert Anthony, *Super Persuasion* (New York: Berkley Publishing Corp., 1973), adapted from pp. 90–91.
4. Harold H. Bloomfield, *Making Peace with Yourself* (New York: Ballantine Books, 1985), adapted from pp. 84–85.

5. Dale Carnegie, *How to Win Friends and Influence People* (New York: Pocket Books, 1936), pp. 41–42.

6. Ibid., pp. 43–44.

Chapter 9

1. Robert M. Bramson, *Coping with Difficult People* (Garden City, NJ: Anchor Press/Doubleday, 1981), adapted from pp. 69–80.

2. Ibid., adapted from pp. 115-128.

Chapter 10

1. Harold Bloomfield, *Making Peace with Your Parents* (New York: Random House, 1983), adapted from pp. 58–59.

2. Leonard Felder, *A Fresh Start* (New York: Signet Books, 1987), adapted from pp. 98–100.

3. Ibid., adapted from pp. 103–105.

4. Charles R. Swindoll, *Living above the Level of Mediocrity* (Waco, TX: Word Books, 1987), p. 100.